The BIG Book of KNOWLEDGE

An Encyclopedia of Questions and Answers

English edition translated from the Italian and edited by Maureen Spurgeon

Brown Watson

ENGLAND

Contents

Editor: Alessandra Gnecchi Ruscone
Production editor: Stefano Sibella
Editorial assistant: Tiziana Campana

Text: Antonella Meiani
Illustrations: Silvia Colombo and Davide Bonadonna

ISBN: 0-7097-1472-6

Il grande libro dei perche
© 2001 Istituto Geografico De Agostini, Novara
© 2002 Brown Watson, English edition
Reprinted 2003(twice), 2005

The Earth

WHAT DOES THE EARTH LOOK LIKE?

The planet Earth is sphere-shaped, slightly flattened at the North and the South Pole. Satellite photographs show that much of its surface is covered by seas and oceans, separating the continents with their mountains, open plains, forests, rivers and lakes. The solid outer surface of the Earth which forms the continents and the ocean beds is called the Earth's Crust.

● WHO WHAT WHEN HOW ●

Who studies the Earth?

A geologist reconstructs the story of our planet by studying the structure of the Earth's Crust and all that happens as a result.

A geophysicist studies all the natural happenings (phenomena) which take place in the atmosphere, on the Earth's surface and inside the planet.

A geographer studies and maps out Earth's natural features – mountains, rivers, lakes, etc. – and man-made additions, such as roads, bridges and canals.

THE BLUE PLANET

Earth is called the Blue Planet because, seen from Space, it looks blue. The waters of the seas and oceans cover about two thirds of the Earth's surface.

Satellite picture of Hong Kong and the coast of Southern China.

FACTS·AND·FIGURES

- Scientists believe that the Earth, like all planets in the Solar System, began to form about 4600 million years ago.

- The diameter of Earth measures 12757km; the distance between the poles is about 12714km.

- The surface of the Earth above sea level is about 149,600,000 square kilometres.

- The combined expanse of the oceans is about 360,650,000 square kilometres.

AN ANCIENT BELIEF

People once believed that the Earth was flat, surrounded by water and deserts.

THE EARTH'S CRUST

The Continental Crust which forms Earth's dry land is thick, but consists of light rock. It is thickest beneath the mountain chains.
The Oceanic Crust which constitutes the ocean beds is composed of heavy rocks but is thinner.

HAS THE EARTH ALWAYS BEEN AS WE KNOW IT?

When Earth first began, the land formed one huge continent. In time, this gradually separated and spread out, slowly becoming the land masses and countries which we know today. This phenomenon is called the Continental Drift.

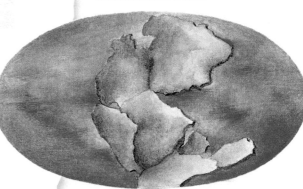

Earth 200 million years ago. Dry land formed one continent called the Pangea which slowly divided itself into two.

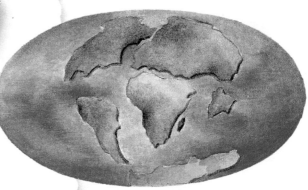

Earth 65 million years ago. Earthquakes and volcanic eruptions divide the two continents into smaller parts.

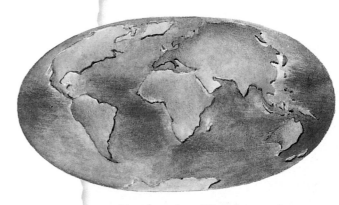

Earth today. The six continents as we know them.

WHAT IS INSIDE THE EARTH?

The Earth is made of layers of rock which surround a nucleus. The layer on the outside is called the Earth's Crust and is a thin layer of solid rock. Under this is the Earth's Mantle, a mass of rock fused together. Deep inside the Earth is the nucleus, or core. The outer part of the nucleus consists of liquid rock, whilst the inside is solid. This is also the hottest because it is under the most pressure. The deeper inside the Earth, the greater the temperature.

THE MAGMA

The outer part of the Earth's Mantle consists of a dense, glutinous mass of fused rock. This is the magma, on which the Earth's Crust 'floats'. The Magma is constantly moving and sometimes bursts out of volcanoes.

Earth's Crust: 35km

THE THICKNESS OF THE EARTH'S CRUST

The Earth's Crust is about 35km thick on average. Beneath mountain chains it can be as thick as 70 km.

● WHO WHAT WHEN HOW ●

What are the most precious stones?

When the magma cools, the material which it contains solidifies in the form of crystals. Precious stones (or 'gems') are crystals with particular characteristics of colour, hardness and the way they can reflect the light. They are cut in such a way as to highlight these qualities and are used in making jewellery.

Diamond

Internal nucleus: 6300km / 4000°C

External nucleus: 5100km / 3600°C

Mantle: 2900km / 3000°C

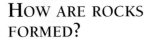

Q·U·I·Z

1) Where is the Earth's crust thickest?
❏ under the sea   ❏ beneath mountains
❏ on the land

2) What is the hardest natural mineral?
❏ diamond   ❏ steel   ❏ bone

3) What is the hottest part of the Earth?
❏ internal nucleus   ❏ external nucleus
❏ the mantle

4) Have a guess! Which planet is as big as the internal nucleus of the Earth?
❏ Mars   ❏ Pluto   ❏ Jupiter

5) Which precious stone is green in colour?
❏ topaz   ❏ emerald   ❏ sapphire

internal nucleus 4) Mars 5) emerald
1) beneath mountains 2) diamond 3)
Answers

HOW ARE ROCKS FORMED?

The rocks of the Earth's Crust are made up of different combinations of various minerals which have different origins.

Magnetic or igneous rock is formed when the magma cools and solidifies, coming out of volcanoes then rising up towards the Earth's Crust.

Basalt, pumice and granite are all examples of magnetic or igneous rock.

Sedimentary rocks are formed of rocky fragments, remains of animals or plants, which, together with other substances, are carried by water and wind and deposited on the beds of oceans or lakes or on dry land. These remains then become solidified and cemented together, and in time transformed into rock. This is the origin of sandstone, limestone and clay.

Basalt

Sandstone

Gneiss

Pink Marble

Some rocks, following devastation of the Earth's Crust, collapse into the interior of the Earth and because of the heat and the pressure, they become completely changed, transformed into metamorphic rocks. Slate, marble and gneiss are examples of metamorphic rock.

MEASURING THE DEPTH

The deepest well which has ever been dug is recorded at 15km deep – which is shallow compared to the depth of the Earth!

HOW DID THE MOUNTAINS BEGIN?

The Earth's Crust is divided into 17 huge plates called tectonic plates, which fit together rather like pieces in a jigsaw puzzle. Tectonic plates are in constant movement, because they rest on the magma underneath. These plates slide one against the other, they collide, they move apart. These movements, as well as causing earthquakes, volcanic eruptions and the Continental Drift (separation of the continents), also led to the formation of mountain chains. When two plates press one against the other, the Earth's Crust is pushed up towards the top and forms mountain chains in 'folds'. But when the Crust breaks along cracks or 'fault lines', great blocks of rock are thrown up and form montain chains in 'blocks'.

'BLOCK' MOUNTAINS
The Sierra Nevada in North America is a 'block' mountain chain.

CONE-SHAPED MOUNTAINS AND DOME-SHAPED MOUNTAINS
When magma erupts from volcanoes and solidifies it forms an isolated mountain in the form of a cone. If the magma only erupts within the Earth's Crust without escaping, then this forms a dome-shaped montain.

● WHO WHAT WHEN HOW ●

How is the height of a mountain measured?

To measure the height (or altitude) of a mountain, we take the surface of the sea as a point of reference. When we say, for example, that the mountain K2 is 8616km a.s.l. (above sea level) we refer to the distance between the top of the mountain and the surface of the sea.

WHAT IS A VALLEY?
A valley is a thin basin situated between the base of mountains. Valleys are formed by erosion (or wearing away) caused by ice and the course of water. The shape of a valley depends on how it began.

8

MOUNTAINS IN 'FOLDS'

The Himalayan Mountains were formed by a collision between the plates of India and those on which the rest of Asia rests. From a collision between Africa and Europe originated the Alps, the Apennines, the Pyrenees and the Atlas Mountains.

• The highest mountain is Everest: 8848m. Second highest is K2, with a height of 8616m. Both are in the Himalayas. After numerous attempts, the first to reach the summit of Everest were the New Zealander Edmund Hillary and the Nepalese Sherpa Tensing in 1953.

• The first man to climb Everest alone was the Italian Rheinhold Messner in 1980. He was also the first mountaineer to climb all 14 mountains higher than 8000m without oxygen cylinders – a truly remarkable achievement.

• The most extensive mountain chain in the world is the Andes in South America, with a length of 7200km.

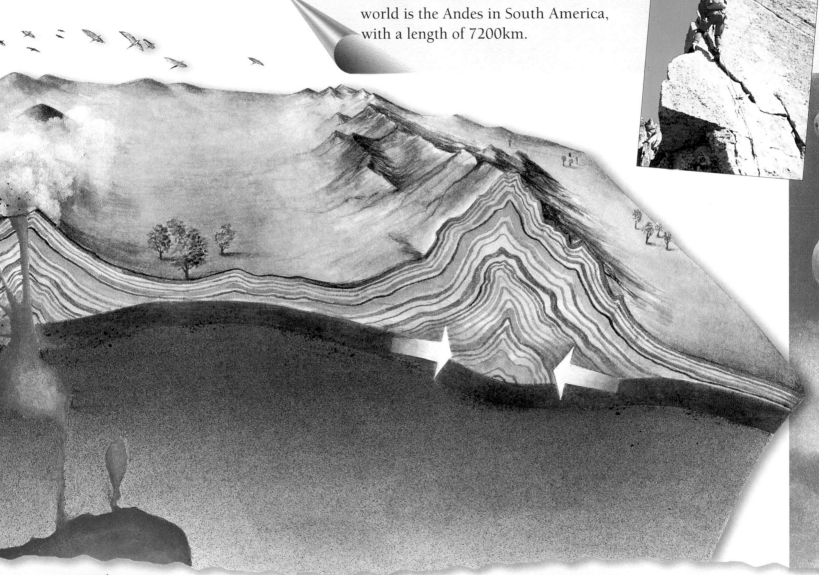

A glacier valley is formed by the slow advance of a glacier and is formed like a letter U – steep sides and a flat base.

A river valley is excavated by the course of a river or waterfall. Its shape is like a letter V – sloping sides and a narrow base.

IS THE EARTH STILL CHANGING?

When we look at the landscape, it all seems quite still and unaltered. But, very, very slowly, Earth is continually changing. The surface of the Earth changes position following the movements of the tectonic plates. It would take many, many millions of years, for example, for North and South America to separate at Panama, or for Africa to break away from Asia at Suez. Volcanic eruptions, earthquakes and floods change the appearance of the Earth and the Oceanic Crust. The rain, the rivers, the seas and ice all erode or wear away the rocks, taking away debris and putting this in different places, thus changing the appearance of the landscape.

'OLD' AND 'YOUNG' MOUNTAINS

'Young' mountains are those which formed just a few million years ago. These have pointed peaks. 'Older' mountains have more rounded peaks, due to erosion caused by ice and wind.

ROUND STONES

The continual coming and going of sea waves or the flowing of rivers moulds stones in the water, making them smooth, flat and rounded.

● WHO WHAT WHEN HOW ●

How is sand formed?

The sand on our beaches originates from the crushing of rocks, due to rain, wind, the seas and rivers. The colour of sand depends on the rocks from which it originates. For example, the sand near a coral reef is white or pinky-white, whilst sand near volcanoes is dark grey.

AVALANCHES

Sometimes, because of sudden changes of temperature, great blocks of snow or ice break away from mountains and descend to the bottom at speed. This is an avalanche.

LANDSLIDES

Landslides are caused by heavy rainfall or sea waves seeping into the earth and causing a sudden collapse of a large area of land. Landslides can also be triggered by an earthquake.

WHY ARE THERE DIFFERENT TYPES OF COASTLINE?

The coast is where the land and the sea meet. Different types of coastline depend on the type of rock and the force of the sea waves. The coastal landscape is constantly changing because it is continually being moulded by the sea.

The rocky walls rising up from the sea become eroded by the waves and these result in caves and creeks or inlets.

Fjords are submerged glacier valleys flooded by water and forming deep inlets in the coastline of Scandinavia.

When a sea or a river deposits fine materials along the coast, these deposits form low, sandy beaches.

WHAT IS AN EARTHQUAKE?

The tectonic plates which comprise the Earth's Crust are in continuous movement. They press one against the other, or they move apart, sometimes moving in opposite directions. As they rub against each other, this slows down their movement, causing an accumulation of an enormous amount of energy. When the two plates finally move, this energy is suddenly released and shakes with enormous vibrations (seismic waves). These vibrations shake the Earth's surface, causing an earthquake. The intensity of the earthquake can be great enough to destroy an entire city, causing death and injury to many victims.

WHERE DO EARTHQUAKES HAPPEN?

Most earthquakes occur along the edges of the tectonic plates and around the fault lines - that is, along the breaks of the Earth's Crust. These areas which we call 'seismic zones' are Japan, Central Asia, Southeast Europe and the U.S.A. (especially California).

HYPOCENTRE AND EPICENTRE

The point at which the seismic wave originates is called the hypocentre, or focus, and is below ground. The epicentre is the point in the Earth's surface which corresponds to the focus.

WHAT IS A GLACIER?

Glaciers cover more than one tenth of the Earth's surface. Glaciers are enormous masses of compressed ice and form in cold zones, at the North and South Poles and on high mountains, where the quantity of snow which accumulates in a year is more than the amount which melts in the heat from the Sun. Mountain glaciers can cause great erosion. Their slow movements down towards the base of the mountain claws away at the rocks and when they meet cracks, they form deep crevasses, hollowing out wide valleys and depositing debris downhill.

- Glaciers cover almost 14 million square kilometres of the Earth's surface.

- The 'fastest-moving' ice is the Columbia Glacier in Alaska which moves about 20m per day. Alpine glaciers 'travel' about 50m in one year.

- The widest glacier (4780m) is in the Antarctic.

- An alpine glacier forms in a time scale which can be from 2 to 20 years.

- The longest iceberg is the Lambert-Fisher Ice Passage in the Australian Antarctic which covers at least 700km.

WHAT IS AN ICEBERG?

Icebergs are fragments of the ice cap which break away from the glacial coast due bombardment of sea waves. Icebergs can become transported by the wind and the sea current. Some can take up to ten years to melt.

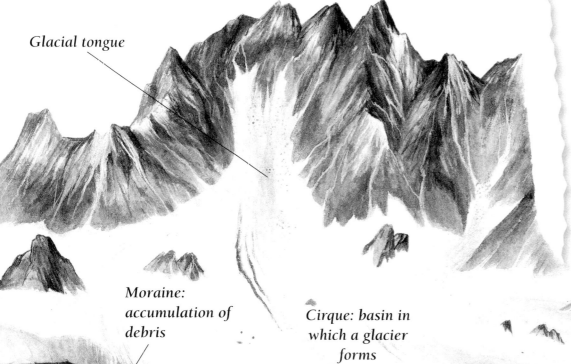

Glacial tongue

Moraine: accumulation of debris

Cirque: basin in which a glacier forms

Front/brow of glacier

WHY DO VOLCANOES ERUPT?

Beneath the Earth's Crust the rocks, melted by heat, form magma, a gleaming-hot liquid mass. When the magma rises up from the depths of the Earth towards the surface, it escapes through a volcano, and there is an eruption. From the mouth (or crater) of the volcano there escapes a flow of lava, often together with steam, cinders, dust and lava fragments (lapilli). When the lava spurts out from the crater of the volcano, it is red and very, very hot (1100°!) and destroys everything it comes in contact with. As it flows the lava cools very, very slowly and solidifies around the volcano, becoming grey or black in colour.

• WHO WHAT WHEN HOW •

What are geysers?

Geysers are jets of steam coming from the inside of the Earth. These jets can reach about 10m high. They are caused by the magma heating up water in an underground chamber to boiling point, with the steam escaping through cracks in the Earth's surface.

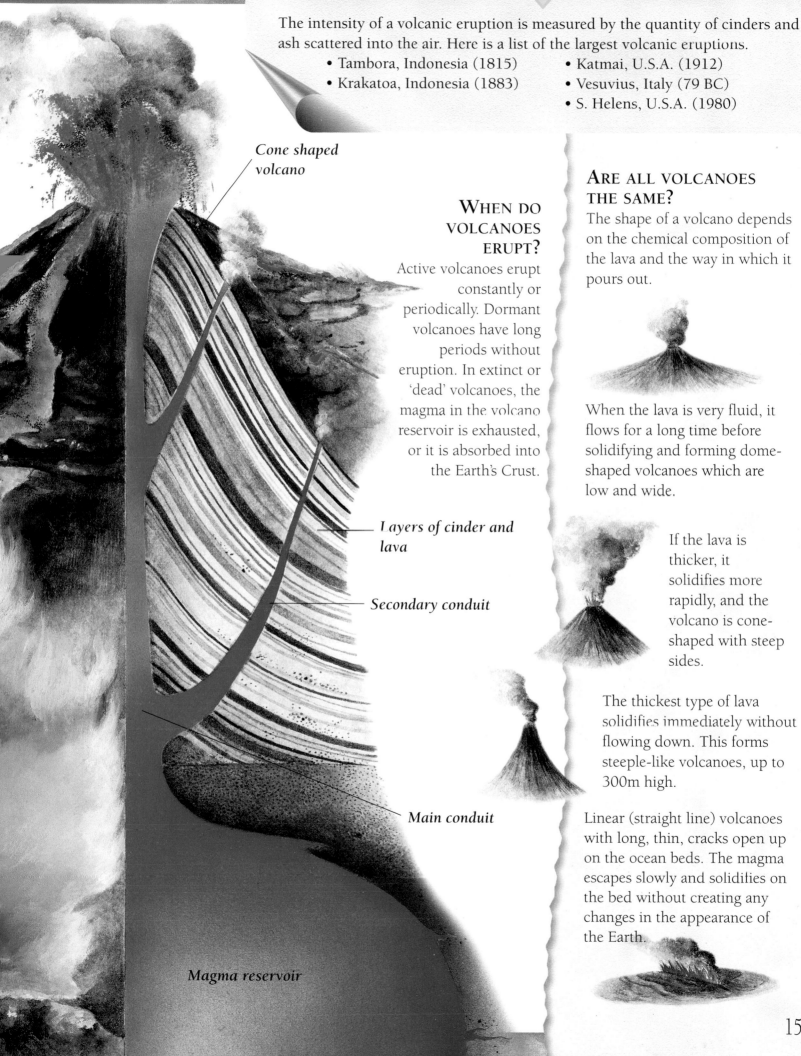

FACTS·AND·FIGURES

The intensity of a volcanic eruption is measured by the quantity of cinders and ash scattered into the air. Here is a list of the largest volcanic eruptions.

- Tambora, Indonesia (1815)
- Krakatoa, Indonesia (1883)
- Katmai, U.S.A. (1912)
- Vesuvius, Italy (79 BC)
- S. Helens, U.S.A. (1980)

Cone shaped volcano

WHEN DO VOLCANOES ERUPT?

Active volcanoes erupt constantly or periodically. Dormant volcanoes have long periods without eruption. In extinct or 'dead' volcanoes, the magma in the volcano reservoir is exhausted, or it is absorbed into the Earth's Crust.

Layers of cinder and lava

Secondary conduit

Main conduit

Magma reservoir

ARE ALL VOLCANOES THE SAME?

The shape of a volcano depends on the chemical composition of the lava and the way in which it pours out.

When the lava is very fluid, it flows for a long time before solidifying and forming dome-shaped volcanoes which are low and wide.

If the lava is thicker, it solidifies more rapidly, and the volcano is cone-shaped with steep sides.

The thickest type of lava solidifies immediately without flowing down. This forms steeple-like volcanoes, up to 300m high.

Linear (straight line) volcanoes with long, thin, cracks open up on the ocean beds. The magma escapes slowly and solidifies on the bed without creating any changes in the appearance of the Earth.

15

How did the oceans form?

The Earth began as a cloud of dust and hot, shining gas. When our planet began to cool, its surface solidified, surrounded by clouds of water vapour. When this vapour condensed (changed into liquid) and began to fall like rain, seas and oceans formed in the hollows of the Earth's surface. Oceans are huge expanses of water which separate the Earth's continents. The largest ocean is the Pacific Ocean, second the Atlantic and third largest the Indian Ocean. Seas are smaller expanses of water, almost always flowing either into oceans or other seas.

- As well as being the largest ocean, the Pacific is also the deepest. Challenger Deep in the Marianna Trench reaches a depth of 1103m!
- The most extensive sea is the South China Sea, covering an area of 3,447,000 square kilometres.
- In the Pacific Ocean is the point furthest from any land, a distance of 2575km

Why are the seas salty?
The waters of the seas and the oceans are always salty, because they are rich in mineral salts and especially sodium chloride, which is the salt used in cooking.

WHAT IS UNDER THE SEA?

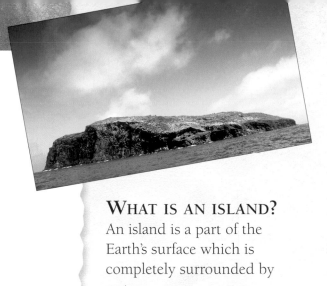

On the beds of oceans and seas there are mountain chains, volcanoes, valleys and deep chasms. The Continental Crust is connected to the ocean by the Continental Shelf, a band of rock which surrounds all the continents, to a maximum depth of 200m. The sea bed then makes a large dip, with the Continental Escarpment (steep slope) which reaches a depth of 3000m. This is where the abyssal plain begins, with volcanoes, ocean trenches and ocean ridges - long mountain chains from which seeps the magma coming from the depths of the Earth. Each ocean ridge matches the edges of two tectonic plates.

WHAT IS AN ISLAND?
An island is a part of the Earth's surface which is completely surrounded by water.

Continental islands are joined under the sea to the Continental Crust.

An oceanic island is actually the peak of a mountain or a part of the Ocean Crust, often from an underwater volcano.

Atolls are found in tropical seas. These are islands which consist of coral reefs that have formed around the craters of volcanoes which have collapsed.

Continental Platform

Continental Escarpment

Abyssal Plain

Ocean Trench

Ocean Ridge

HOW DO WAVES FORM?

Waves are caused by the wind which blows on the seas and the oceans. The more intense the wind, the higher the waves. The water stores up the energy of the wind and releases it into the surrounding air, which begins the movement of the waves: that is why there are sometimes waves when there is no wind blowing. The height of a wave is measured from the highest point on the surface of the sea. The further the wave from the point at which the wind originated, the less its height. Waves move only on the surface of the sea. Below 200m, there is no movement.

The Moon, with its own force of gravity, acts like of a magnet on the waters of the Earth. It is this which causes the rising and falling of the level of the sea, and so high and low tides.

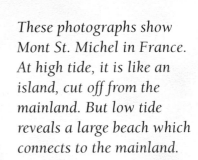

These photographs show Mont St. Michel in France. At high tide, it is like an island, cut off from the mainland. But low tide reveals a large beach which connects to the mainland.

● WHO WHAT WHEN HOW ●

What is an undersea earthquake?

An undersea earthquake is an earthquake which happens at the bottom of an ocean. This creates enormous sea waves called *tsunami* which travel at speeds reaching over 700 kilometres per hour. Near the coast, these sea waves reach heights of about 30m high and break on the shore.

WHAT IS A GROTTO?

Grottos are underwater cavities excavated from the rocks by the effect of erosion. There are many different types of grotto. Some are excavated by the rain which seeps into the cracks of the Earth, others are formed by streams of lava which flow underground. Grottos are also made by sea waves which beat against the rock or where the water bores under the ice. Finally there are those grottos formed by the wind which, with the force of the grains of sand which it brings with it, wears the rock away.

WHAT ARE STALAGTITES AND STALAGMITES?

Grottos begin by rain falling on chalky soil. The rain drips inside, and calcium carbonate (chalk) is dissolved in it. As these chalky drops dry out and build up, they gradually form long, icicle-like deposits hanging from the roof. These are stalagtites. Stalagmites rise up, as a result of chalky drops dripping on the grotto floor.

• Reseau Jean Bernard in France is the deepest grotto in the world (1602m).

• The longest stalagtite is in Spain, in Cueva de Nerja and is 28m long.

• The highest stalagmite in the world measures over 32m and is in the grotto Kràsnohorska in the Czech Republic.

HOW DOES A RIVER BEGIN?

The waters of rivers come from two sources - springs, where the rainwater which penetrates the earth gushes up to the surface, and from the melting of ice which flows down to a lower level, like rain. Rivers usually begin in hills and in mountains. In the first part of the river, because of the strong pull of Earth's gravity, its course is swift and raging, and so the water wears away the rock and digs out its course to form a valley. On the level the river slows down and proceeds with wide curves, called meanders. On its way, the river receives the waters of smaller rivers, its tributaries. The route of the river finishes at its mouth, where its waters flow into the sea.

THE COURSE

The amount of water in a river is not always the same. It increases when there is heavy rain and when the Sun melts ice in the spring. During the summer, some rivers dry up completely, when their waters evaporate in the heat of the Sun.

THE RIVER BED

The bed of the river is continually shaped and moulded by the flowing water, wearing the earth away at certain points, and depositing debris in others. In this way, the water gradually forms new bends in the river, too.

● WHO WHAT WHEN HOW ●

Why is sea water salty and not river water?

In fact, river water does contain salt which it absorbs from the rocks over which it flows. However, the quantity is so low that it cannot be tasted. When a river flows into the sea, its waters evaporate, releasing this small quantity of salt to make the waters of the seas and the oceans salty.

HOW IS THE MOUTH OF A RIVER FORMED?

The mouth of a river can be a delta or an estuary, depending on the force of the current of the sea and on the quantity of debris transported by its waters. At the mouth, the waters of a river becomes more salty as it mixes with the salty waters of the sea.

HOW IS A LAKE FORMED?

Lakes are expanses of water, generally calm, which fill up hollows of the Earth. Their appearance depends on the different ways in which they began. For instance, lakes can fill the craters of ancient extinct volcanoes, or a hollow in a glacier. If a large section of ice in a glacier becomes loosened, this can lead to something like a landslip, which may block the flow of a river, or accumulate the debris near the shore of a sea. The water of a lake can be fed by underground streams or from a river which enters into the lake as intake and cannot escape as outake.

WHY DO LAKES FORM?
The form of a lake depends on its origins.

Volcanic lakes are small and have the circular shape of craters.

Glacial lakes, those which are formed in high regions of a glacier, have a circular shape.
Those which have a thin, long shape are found in glacier valleys.

Coastal lakes, which are parallel to the coast, are formed when the sand holds back the water of a river as it flows towards the sea.

WHY ARE ARTIFICIAL LAKES MADE?
Large quantities of water can be collected in an artificial lake. The water can then be converted to power hydroelectric stations, irrigation plants and water distribution systems in built-up areas.

23

WHAT IS THE ATMOSPHERE?

No life on our planet would be possible without the thick layer of air which surrounds it, and which we call the atmosphere. It is the presence of oxygen in the atmosphere which allows living things to breathe and which protects the Earth from the rays of the Sun by maintaining the right temperature. The atmosphere is about 1000km thick and is divided into five layers, which have different characteristics. The layer nearest to the Earth's surface is called the troposphere, from the Greek word *tropos* which means 'movement'. This is the most turbulent layer and is where our weather comes from. The gases which make up the atmosphere become thinner and thinner the higher up they are, before reaching Outer Space.

The troposphere is in contact with Earth's surface. Here, the air is composed of nitrogen, oxygen, carbon dioxide and thin gases and water vapour. This is where the wind, the rain and snow begin. In the higher zone of the troposphere the temperature reaches about -70°C.

The mesosphere slows down fragments of heavenly bodies, such as shooting stars and meteorites as they fall to Earth from Outer Space. As they fall, these fragments disintegrate and burn out.

In the stratosphere we find a thin layer of oxygen, the gas which protects Earth from the harmful rays of the Sun. Pollution on Earth risks the destruction of this layer, which in turn risks the health of all living things. Its temperature is very low.

● WHO WHAT WHEN HOW ●

How is it that the atmosphere does not crush us?

There are about 15 tonnes of air pressing down on us from above, yet we are not aware of it! The air does not crush us because its pressure is distributed evenly on our bodies, and is balanced by the air which is inside each one of us.

T·E·S·T

Does air weigh anything?
Place a ruler on a table so that one end juts out over the edge. Cover the part on the table with a large sheet of paper and smooth the paper down firmly. What do you think will happen if you hit the edge of the ruler? That the paper will lift up and fly off the table?
Try it, and you will see that the paper does not lift at all, due to the weight of the air on its surface!

IN FLIGHT

To avoid the effects of different atmospheric disturbances, aeroplanes fly at the top limit of the troposphere, 10km from the Earth, where the air is clearer and calmer.

In the ionosphere, the temperature can reach about 1000°C. This is where artificial satellites and space stations are put into orbit.

In the exosphere, the air is always more rareified (thinner) and the temperature reaches about 2000°C.

WHY IS THE SKY BLUE?

The light from the Sun may look white, but actually light is composed of seven colours, the same colours which form a rainbow. The rays of the Sun, when they enter the atmosphere, split up and go in different directions. Some colours become reduced. Others are reflected on to our eyes and others are visible only from some positions. The sky appears blue because it reflects only this colour; so our eyes only see the blue. At dawn and at sunset, the sky appears red because the light, which comes from the Sun low on the horizon, spreads into the atmosphere in a different way so only the rays of that colour reach our eyes.

WHY DOES A RAINBOW APPEAR?

The phenomenon of a rainbow also depends on the spread of light. After a storm raindrops remain suspended in the air. The light from the Sun crosses through drops and its light becomes split up into its seven colours, forming a coloured arch in the sky. The colours of the rainbow are always in the same order: red, orange, green, blue, indigo, violet.

• WHO WHAT WHEN HOW •

Why is space dark?

When we go into a cinema or darkened room, we can see rays of light with tiny little grains dancing around. These are specks of dust. Without the atmosphere, and therefore without these specks of dust, light could not spread; that is why the image of space shows us the planets immersed in darkness.

WHY DOES THE WIND BLOW?

When the air becomes heated up by the Sun, it becomes lighter and rises up high. Cold air, being heavier, descends lower. These movements of hot and cold air which take place in the atmosphere are continuous. When the hot air rises, cold air descends lower and takes the place of the hot air and this begins to form wind. Weather experts study carefully the formation of winds and predict weather conditions in different parts of the world. They use satellite images which show the Earth's surface as covered by masses of cloud in constant movement.

FACTS·AND·FIGURES

Here is a scale of hurricanes according to their intensity.

Grade	Wind speed (km per hr.)	Damage
1	120-153	minimal
2	154-177	moderate
3	178-209	extensive
4	210-249	extreme
5	over 250	catastrophic

WHAT IS A TROPICAL CYCLONE?

A tropical cyclone is a violent storm which forms on oceans in tropical regions. Water vapour and the hot air rising up rapidly from the sea forms a whirlwind of dense cloud which spins around a centre called the 'eye' of the cyclone and which moves at high speed. If the cyclone reaches the land, it causes rain, violent winds and blows high waves, destroying everything in its path.

WHY DO CLOUDS FORM?

The heat from the Sun makes water from rivers, lakes, seas and oceans evaporate. This water vapour rises up into the sky and when this meets colder air, it condenses - that means, the water vapour turns back into little drops which form a cloud. But sometimes, clouds form when hot air meets the mountains, rises up the slopes, and then condenses.

ARE ALL CLOUDS THE SAME?

Different clouds can be recognized by their shape and their distance from the Earth.

Cirrus: Small clouds, white, thin and sometimes in strips, which can be a sign of rain.

Cirrocumulus: Characteristic 'mackerel sky' clouds, made up of small crystals of ice. They are a sign of cold weather.

Cirrostratus: Cloud in the form of a see-through, wispy layer and can be a sign of rain or snow.

Altostratus: An expanse of white or grey cloud which brings rain.

Altocumulus: These have an irregular shape, and can be white, greyish, in layers or all over.

Nimbostratus: Typical rain clouds, dark and grey.

Stratocumulus: Grey clouds, round and with bulges. They bring light rain.

Stratus: A low, grey, thick layer of cloud bringing drizzle and sleet.

Cumulus: White clouds, piled up high. When these are small it is a sign of fine weather.

Cumulonimbus This looks like a tower, dark at the base. It bring storms.

● WHO WHAT WHEN HOW ●

How does mist form?

Mist is made up of fine little drops of water which originate from the condensation of water vapour near the ground. It forms when the air, heavy with water vapour, cools rapidly because of a sudden change in temperature.

WHY DOES IT RAIN AND SNOW?

The drops which form clouds are in continuous movement: when these drops meet, they join together to form bigger, heavier drops, which the air can no longer hold, and so they fall in the form of rain. As each drop falls it grows in size by a million times. The drops which grow also join together during their fall. Rain forms due to the presence of specks of dust. The drops of vapour cluster around these particles and grow larger as a result. If the cloud cools a lot, the drops form crystals of ice which fall as snow.

WHAT IS HAIL?

Hail forms when the highest part of the clouds are in a very cold zone of the atmosphere. Raindrops fall, but violent currents of air sweep them up higher, where they join with other drops, and then down again where they join more drops. When the drops become heavy lumps of ice they fall in the form of hail.

If you were to open a hailstone, you would see that it is composed of different layers of ice, due to the many journeys it has made.

• WHO WHAT WHEN HOW •

How is snow made?

Snow falls in soft flakes joined lightly together, each flake composed of tiny crystals which form due to the cold. All snowflakes have a geometrical shape of five points, but each one is different to another. When snowflakes accumulate, the snow becomes packed together, because its own weight squeezes out the air from the interior of the flakes.

HOW DOES THE EARTH MOVE?

The Earth moves in two ways - it spins on its own, and at the same time, it travels around (orbits) the Sun. The Earth's rotation determines the day and the night, the orbit around the Sun, and the change in the seasons. The rotation of the Earth is on its axis, an imaginary line, slightly tilted and which links the North and South Poles. One rotation of the Earth on its axis lasts 24 hours and goes in an anti-clockwise direction. The journey of the Earth around the Sun follows an elliptic (oval) orbit, also in an anti-clockwise direction. The journey of the Earth around the Sun lasts 365 hours and six hours.

THE CALENDAR
The year is divided into 12 months. One month is based on the time it takes for the Moon to make an orbit around the Earth (29 and a half days).

● WHO WHAT WHEN HOW ●

What is a leap year?

It takes the Earth 365 days and six hours to orbit around the Sun. The six extra hours cannot be counted on the calendar. So, to keep an accurate count, we add an extra day at the end of February every four years. This day is the sum total of the six odd hours multiplied by four. So, there is a leap year every four years which has 366 days.

To draw a model of Earth's orbit, take a piece of card and fix two pins in the centre, as shown in the picture. Then take a pencil, and loop an elastic band around this and the two pins to form a triangle. Keeping the elastic band tight, draw a complete circle around the pins with the pencil; you will draw an ellipse on the cardboard - a circle shape which is slightly flattened

WHY IS THERE DAY AND NIGHT?

The word 'day' means the time the Earth takes to make a complete rotation on its axis, including both the hours of daylight (day) and the hours of darkness (night). During the rotation, the Sun lights up one half of the Earth at a time, and so in one half there is day and the opposite half, the half in darkness, there is night. The day and the night do not last the same amount of time in different parts of the world. Because the Earth's axis is always tilted, our picture shows what happens when the Earth is in this position in relation to the Sun.

WHY DO THE SEASONS CHANGE?

When the Earth travels around the Sun, it is slightly tilted on its axis. This means that its upper half, the Northern Hemisphere, has an exposure to the Sun which is different to that in the bottom half, the Southern Hemisphere. The alternation of the seasons depends on these positions. In the summer, the rays fall almost perpendicular to the hemisphere with the most sunlight, and the day lasts longer than the night. In the opposite hemisphere, it is winter: the rays of the Sun fall obliquely (at an angle) and the day is shorter than the night. In the autumn and in spring, the day and the night lasts approximately the same amount of time. At the Poles during the summer it is always day, whilst in the winter, it is always night.

HOW MANY SEASONS ARE THERE?

The year is divided into four seasons, each lasting three months. Near the Poles, there are only two seasons, winter and summer, each lasting six months. At the Equator, there are no seasons. Day and night always lasts the same, with frequent rains and it is always hot.

In the Northern Hemisphere summer begins on the 21st June and the part of the Earth in the light of the Sun is more extensive than the part in the dark. During this time, the North Pole is always lit by the Sun, whilst the South Pole is always in darkness. In the opposite hemisphere, the winter begins.

In the Northern Hemisphere, autumn begins on 23 September. The hours of daylight are the same as the hours of darkness. We call this the Autumn Equinox.

Q·U·I·Z

1) *Is the distance from a geographical point to the Equator called latitude or longitude?*

2) *The climate of the seasons is largely influenced by latitude or longitude?*

3) *How many parallels are there?*

4) *How many meridian lines are there?*

5) *As the Earth travels around the Sun, does the tilt of its axis change direction?*

Answers

1) *Latitude* 2) *Latitude* 3) 180 4) 360 5) *No*

THE HEMISPHERES

The Equator is an imaginary line at an equal distance between the two Poles and which divides the Earth into two hemispheres - the Northern (or Boreal) Hemisphere and the Southern (or Austral) Hemisphere.

MERIDIANS AND PARALLELS

On a map, the Earth is criss-crossed with imaginary lines, so that we can locate the position of any point on the planet. Parallels are the horizontal lines and are parallel to the Equator, and meridians are the lines which go from the North Pole to the South, dividing the Earth into equal segments.

The 21st March is the first day of Spring in the Northern Hemisphere. As on 23 September, the day and the night lasts the same number of hours. We call this the Spring Equinox.

In the Northern Hemisphere, winter begins on 21st December. The darkened zone is furthest away from the Sun. The North Pole is dark and the South Pole is in the light. Summer time begins in the Southern Hemisphere.

DOES THE SUN ALWAYS SET?

At the Arctic Circle, it is possible to see the Sun at midnight on 21st June. On this day, the Sun descends on the horizon, but does not set.

WHY IS IT ALWAYS COLD AT THE POLES?

As well as light, the rays of the Sun give heat to the Earth. The shorter the distance from the Sun, the more heat there is from it. If the rays fall perpendicular (straight down) on the Earth's surface, this creates a climate which is always hot. If the rays fall at an angle, they cover a greater distance and so the force of heat is a lot less. That is why, although both Poles get light from the Sun, they get little heat from it. Here, the temperature ranges from 0° to -80°C and ice covers the ground all year round.

CAN PEOPLE LIVE AT THE POLES?

The Arctic consists of the North Arctic Sea, permanently iced over, and the Northern part of America, Europe and Asia. Here live the Lapps, the Inuit (Eskimos) and the Greenlanders.

The animals which are able to live in polar climate are polar bears, seals, walruses, marine elephants, penguins and whales.

34

The Universe

WHAT IS A STAR?

The stars that we see shining in the sky at night are spheres of very hot gas which give off a strong light. For a star to shine, it has to reach a temperature of around 10 million degrees Centigrade! The colour of a star depends on its size and its temperature. The largest are also the hottest, and shine with a blue light. Some smaller stars shine with a white light, some yellow, others orange or pink. The different ways in which they shine also depends on their distance from Earth. The closer the star, the more clearly we see its light. Smaller stars have an average diameter of a few thousand kilometres. The diameter of the largest stars can reach up to three billion kilometres!

BILLIONS OF STARS

Scientists estimate that there are 200 billion, billion stars. About 3000 can be seen with the naked eye in each hemisphere of the Earth. Seen from our planet, the stars all seem to be at the same distance. In fact, they are at many different distances.

• HOW WHY WHEN •

What is a Light Year?

The unit of measurement used to calculate enormous distances in space is the Light Year – that is, the distance which light travels in one year. One Light Year is equal to 9460 billion kilometres. Try to work out the diameter of the Milky Way (100,000 Light Years) in kilometres, and you will get a number which you would not be able to pronounce!

FACTS·AND·FIGURES

- The star nearest to us, excluding the Sun, is Proxima Centurai, which is 4.3 Light Years from Earth.
- The largest star is the supergiant Betelgeuse which is 520 Light Years from us. Its diameter is about 400 times greater than that of the Sun.
- The star which looks brightest from Earth is Sirius – its name means 'shining'. It is 8.6 Light Years from our planet.

NEBULAE

Nebulae are clouds of dust and gas in which there may be the origins of stars. Sometimes, they are the remains of 'dying' stars. Some nebulae shine due to the presence of very hot stars. Others are dark and quite dense.

HOW IS A STAR BORN?

The life of a star begins at the heart of a nebula. Together, gas and dust form a nucleus which is always very dense and hot. When the temperature reaches about 10 million degrees Centigrade, the nucleus ignites and the star begins to shine, burning hydrogen, which is one of its basic elements, for billions of years.

A star of great dimensions (supergiant) burns very quickly and in the end explodes.
From this explosion there forms a supernova.
A star of medium dimensions, for example a 'yellow dwarf' like our Sun, once it exhausts the hydrogen, becomes bigger and brighter, changing into a 'red giant'.
Gradually, its nucleus shrinks again, slowly becoming cooler and heavier. Now the golden star is a 'white dwarf' which will gradually cool down until it is extinguished altogether.

WHAT IS A GALAXY?

A galaxy is a huge mass of stars, gas and dust, all kept together by the force of gravity, and rotating around a central point. In the Universe there are billions of galaxies. A galaxy can comprise between one billion to 100,000 billion stars. There are galaxies of different forms and sizes. The elliptic (oval) galaxy has old stars and is generally large and bright. Spiral galaxies have 'long' arms spiralling out from a central nucleus. Those 'arms' contain mainly new stars, and are where new stars may begin. Irregular galaxies do not have an exact formation. They are usually small and rich in gas and dust.

MASSES AND MASSES OF GALAXIES

Galaxies tend to group together, forming masses of a hundred or a thousand galaxies. Sometimes, these can develop into super-clusters, comprising hundreds of masses!

● HOW WHY WHAT WHEN ●

What is a Black Hole?

The explosion of a big star can generate a Black Hole – that is, a heavenly body in which the force of gravity is so strong that it does not allow anything to escape, not even light. That is why a Black Hole cannot be seen, not even with the most powerful telescope.

BARRED SPIRALS

Some spiral galaxies are cut through with a straight bar of stars at the centre with spiral 'arms' branching off at the end. These galaxies are called 'barred spirals'.

QUASARS

All Quasars (quasi-stellar object) are millions of light years away from Earth. A Quasar looks like a star, but it is widely believed that it is actually the nucleus of a galaxy, with a black hole at the centre.

• The Milky Way, like other galaxies, is rotating slowly around, like a huge ring. It takes 230 million years to make a complete circuit.

• The nearest galaxies to us are the Small Magellanic Cloud and the Large Magellanic Cloud. Smaller than the Milky Way, these are only visible to the naked eye in southern (austral) skies.

• The furthest galaxy visible with the naked eye is Andromeda. Its light takes more than two million years to reach Earth. So, we see it as it was two million years ago.

• The diameter of the Milky Way is about 100,000 Light Years.

WHAT IS THE MILKY WAY?

The Milky Way is our galaxy. It gets its name because in the starry sky, it appears to the naked eye as a milky-white trail. It is a spiral galaxy, with the Sun and other planets in one of its 'arms', that of Orion, which is 33000 Light Years from the centre.

All that we see in the sky with the naked eye belongs to our galaxy, with the exception of three patches which, in fact, are other galaxies.

WHAT ARE COMETS?

Comets are spheres of frozen gases and dust. They travel around the Sun on very long orbits. As it nears the Sun, the heat evaporates the comet's surface and this produces a shining globe of gas and dust around the nucleus and trail of vapour. This trail is pushed away from the Sun by Solar Winds to form the tail of the comet. A comet's tail can be up to hundreds of millions of kilometres long and always goes in the opposite direction to the Sun. The trail and the tail of a comet are visible because both spread the solar light. Slowly, slowly, as the comet draws further away from the Sun, the tail gets shorter until it disappears altogether.

• HOW WHY WHAT WHEN •

When was a Comet last seen?

The larger the comet, the longer its orbit, which can take thousands or millions of years.
Therefore, its appearance is always a big event.
Halley's Comet is the only one which returns every 76 years. Its last sighting was in 1986.

WHAT ARE FALLING STARS?

Falling stars are actually small pieces of rock and metal from a comet. When these enter our atmosphere at high speed, they change into shining, bright vapour and light up the sky with a shining trail.

40

DOUBLE TAIL

The tail of a comet is actually two tails – one, straight and gaseous, and the other, wide and curved, made of dust particles.

• The largest meteorite was found in 1920 in Africa. It weighed about 60 tonnes and measured 2.7 x 2.4 metres.
• The most spectacular crater made by a meteorite is the Devil's Canyon Meteor Crater in Arizona, USA. This has a diameter of more than 1200 metres and is 183 metres deep. It is thought that this crater was made about 50,000 years ago.

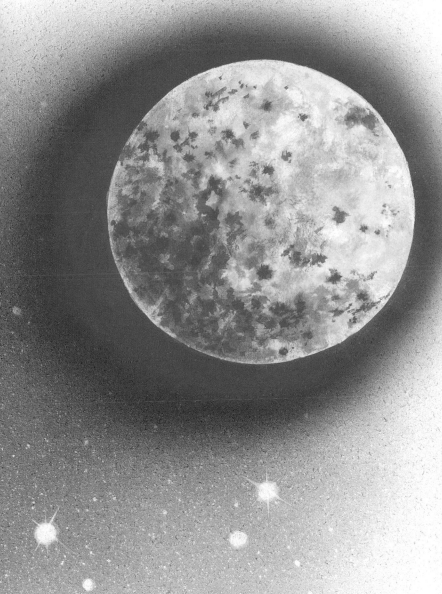

THE SUN CONSUMES COMETS

As they pass near the Sun, a comet loses one centimetre from its external layer per day. So, in time a comet is destined to be consumed completely.

The scientific name for a falling star is a meteor. In August the Earth passes through a trail of meteors, and many 'falling stars' often appear in the night sky at that time. Some of the larger meteors do not disintegrate in the atmosphere, but fall to Earth. These are called meteorites and can be large enough to make enormous craters in the Earth's surface.

WHAT IS THE SUN?

The Sun is a star, an enormous globe of shining gas. At the centre, at a temperature of 15 million degrees Centigrade, are nuclear reactors capable of releasing an enormous quantity of energy. Only the tiniest, smallest part of this energy reaches Earth and this energy is essential to give life to our planet. The Sun is the centre of a system of planets of which Earth is a part. It is about 150 million kilometres away from us. To have some idea of how large the Sun is, imagine a huge container which could hold one million and a half planets as big as the Earth.

THE AGE OF THE SUN

Compared to the age of other stars, the Sun is not all that old. It is a 'yellow dwarf', which came into existence about 5 billion years ago. It will shine for another 5 billion years.

• HOW WHY WHAT WHEN •

What is the speed of light?

Light travels at a speed of 300,000km per second. Even at the distance between the Sun and the Earth at around 150 million kilometres, light takes 8.5 minutes to reach our planet.

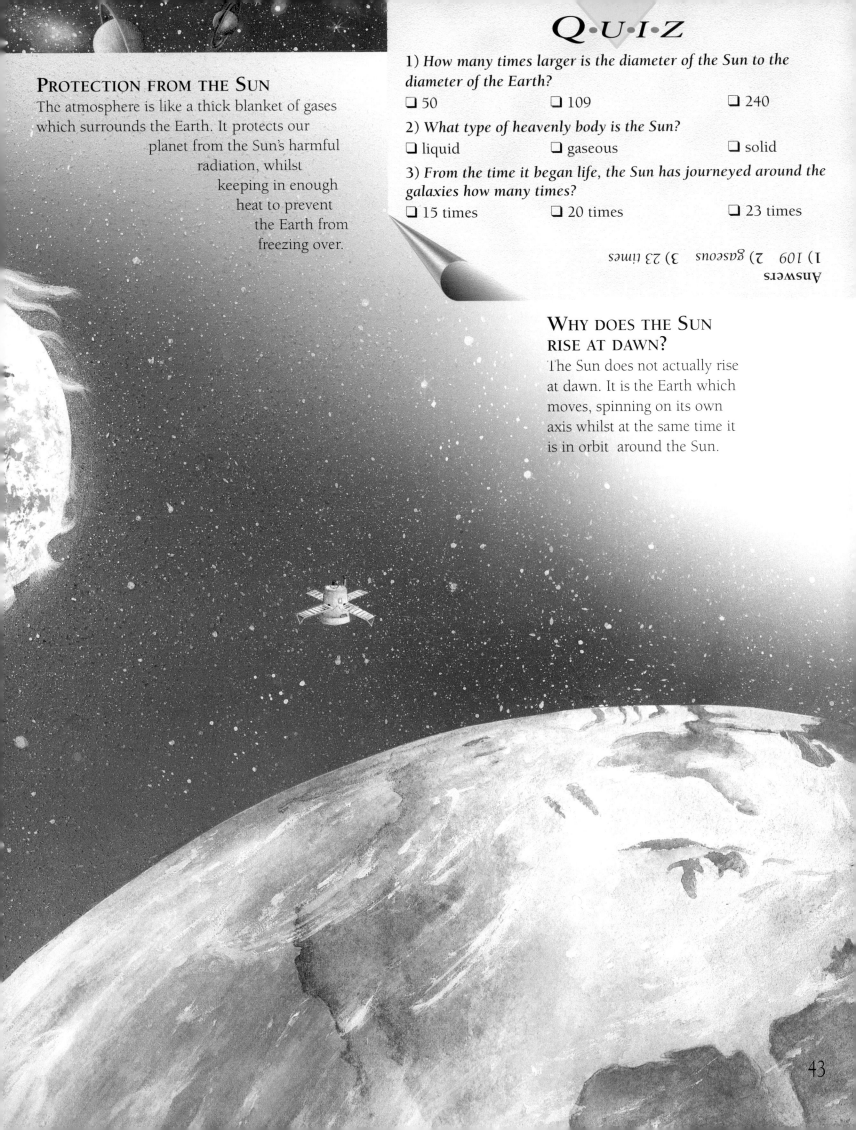

PROTECTION FROM THE SUN

The atmosphere is like a thick blanket of gases which surrounds the Earth. It protects our planet from the Sun's harmful radiation, whilst keeping in enough heat to prevent the Earth from freezing over.

Q·U·I·Z

1) *How many times larger is the diameter of the Sun to the diameter of the Earth?*

❑ 50 ❑ 109 ❑ 240

2) *What type of heavenly body is the Sun?*

❑ liquid ❑ gaseous ❑ solid

3) *From the time it began life, the Sun has journeyed around the galaxies how many times?*

❑ 15 times ❑ 20 times ❑ 23 times

Answers
1) 109   2) gaseous   3) 23 times

WHY DOES THE SUN RISE AT DAWN?

The Sun does not actually rise at dawn. It is the Earth which moves, spinning on its own axis whilst at the same time it is in orbit around the Sun.

43

WHAT IS THERE AT THE CENTRE OF THE SUN?

Like every star at the middle phase of its life, the Sun shines because it is burning the hydrogen contained in its nucleus and which it transforms into another gas, helium. The light and the colour which result from this reaction comes from the nucleus and spreads towards the external part, going through different layers of the Sun until it reaches its Photosphere or visible surface (after 200,000 years!) From here, the light and heat spreads at great speed into the space surrounding it.

THE ROTATION OF THE SUN

The Sun rotates on its own. But, because it is a gaseous body, it does not have a regular speed. It spins round its equator every 25 Earth days, 31 Earth days at its Poles.

Prominence

Photosphere

Nucleus

● HOW WHY WHAT WHEN ●

Is it possible to explore the Sun?

The temperature of the Sun, which, even on the surface, is about 6000°C, makes it impossible for anyone to explore it on site. From Earth, we can only see the Photosphere.
From 1996 the Space Probe Soho has been positioned between the Earth and the Sun, observing the Sun 24 hours a day. It has sent back to Earth a great deal of data about the Sun's activity.

CYCLE OF ACTIVITY

Corona

Activity on the Sun, such as prominences and sunspots, waxes and wanes during the 'Solar Cycle'. Activity reaches a peak every 11 years, when at maximum, the number of sunspots increase.

Chromosphere

Sunspots

The temperature of the Sun

• Nucleus: 15,000,000°C.
The part of the Sun in which hydrogen is transformed into helium generates light and heat.
• The Chromosphere: between 8000 and 20,000°C.
Gaseous, red-hot layer which constitutes the solar atmosphere.
• Photosphere: 5700°C. Luminous surface.
• Corona: 1,000,000°C. The most external zone of the Sun, visible during a Solar Eclipse. It extends for millions of kilometres and the Solar Wind forms from its particles.
• Sunspots. 4500°C. Dark zone of the Photosphere and where the temperature is lower.
• Prominence: more than 10,000°C.
A gas jet which rises for thousands of kilometres.

CONVECTIVE AND RADIATIVE ZONES

The Convective Zone is the layer of the Sun in which bubbles of shining gas transmit energy to the outside. The Radiative Zone is the area where energy passes from the nucleus to the outer layer.

WHAT IS THE SOLAR WIND?

The Corona (outer atmosphere) of the Sun releases a flow of tiny particles which travel through space at speeds of hundreds of kilometres per second in the form of the Solar Wind, which expands into the Solar System.

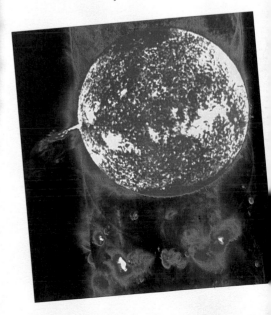

WHAT IS THE SOLAR SYSTEM?

The Sun, with its powerful force of attraction, keeps in orbit around itself 9 planets, including the Earth, 68 listed satellites, countless asteroids, meteors and comets, and a great quantity of dust and gas. Planets are spherical bodies, small and cold. They shine because they reflect the light from the star around which they orbit. Other heavenly bodies called satellites often orbit around planets. There is no life on satellites. Asteroids are minor planets, small and rocky. They orbit around the Sun between Mars and Jupiter, forming a flattened ring with a diameter of 12 billions of kilometres.

• HOW WHY WHAT WHEN •

When did the Universe begin?

According to the most popular theory, the Universe began with a big explosion, the Big Bang, which happened 15 billion years ago. From this began the expansion of the Universe. This expansion continues today, shown by the progressive moving away of galaxies, one from another. The matter from the Big Bang became cooler, little by little, and from this originated the planets, the stars and the galaxies.

THE DIRECTION OF ROTATION

Planets orbit around the Sun, whilst at the same time rotating on their own axis. These rotations are mostly anti-clockwise; only the planet Venus rotates in a clockwise direction.

THINGS·TO·DO

With a light-coloured felt-tipped pen, draw some galaxies of different shapes on a flat blue or black balloon. As you inflate the balloon, you will see, little by little, the galaxies gradually spreading away from each other, as the surface of the balloon expands. Much the same thing happens in the Universe. This is just one model used by scientists to demonstrate the expansion of the Universe.

HOW WAS THE SOLAR SYSTEM BORN?

At least 5 billion years ago, a cloud of gas and dust began to squeeze together, spinning rather like a whirlwind. At the centre of this whirlwind the gas began to thicken, forming a star, the Sun. Away from the centre, the particles continued to spin and to collect together, forming clusters which became bigger and bigger. These were the planets, which then began to orbit around the Sun. From the smaller fragments began the asteroid belt, which also began to orbit around the Sun.

THE SHAPE OF ORBITS

In their journeys around the Sun, planets follow an elliptic (oval) path. Earth's orbit has the shape of a slightly flattened circle.

WHY ARE THE PLANETS DIFFERENT TO EACH OTHER?

Although the nine planets in the Solar System were born at the same time, each one is different to another, in size and its composition. The difference depends on their distance from the Sun and the effects caused by the gravity of the Sun at the moment of the birth of the Solar System. Mercury, Venus, Earth and Mars, the smallest and nearest the Sun, are 'earth' planets, formed of rock and metal. Jupiter, Saturn, Uranus and Neptune, the 'giants', much larger and further away, each have a nucleus of rock wrapped in thick layers of liquid and gas and circled by rings of dust, ice and stones. Pluto, the planet which is furthest from the Sun, is small and icy; some scientists believe that it is not a planet, but a comet.

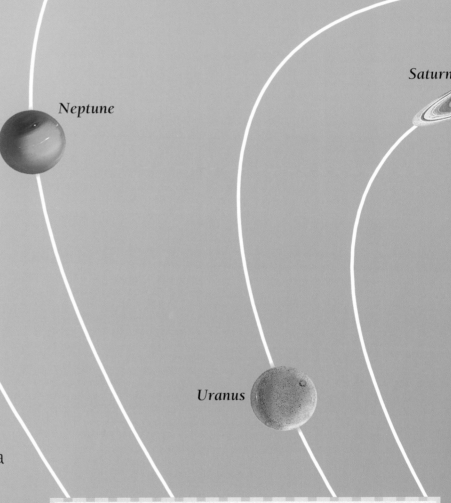

Pluto

Neptune

Saturn

Uranus

● HOW WHY WHAT WHEN ●

Can asteroids fall to Earth?

Some asteroids pass very near to our planet and could even collide with it. However, there is a 'Space Survey Service' called the Spaceguard Foundation, which studies and prevents asteroids from coming too near the Earth. Thanks to the Foundation, it is possible to estimate the path of an asteroid in order to avoid an impact with Earth's surface.

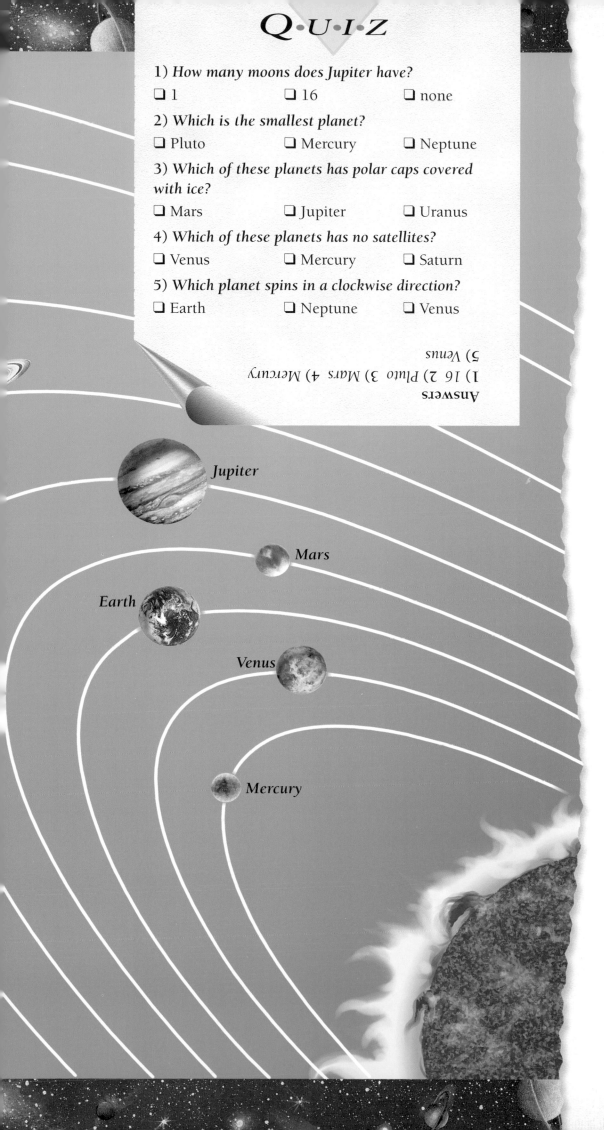

Q·U·I·Z

1) **How many moons does Jupiter have?**
❑ 1   ❑ 16   ❑ none

2) **Which is the smallest planet?**
❑ Pluto   ❑ Mercury   ❑ Neptune

3) **Which of these planets has polar caps covered with ice?**
❑ Mars   ❑ Jupiter   ❑ Uranus

4) **Which of these planets has no satellites?**
❑ Venus   ❑ Mercury   ❑ Saturn

5) **Which planet spins in a clockwise direction?**
❑ Earth   ❑ Neptune   ❑ Venus

Answers
1) 16 2) Pluto 3) Mars 4) Mercury
5) Venus

Jupiter

Mars

Earth

Venus

Mercury

PLANET FACTS

Jupiter is the largest planet in the Solar System – 1400 times the size of Earth.

Mercury is the planet nearest the Sun. It has the shortest orbit. To complete an orbit around the Sun it takes 88 Earth days.

Saturn is surrounded by many rings and spins at high speed on its axis; a day on Saturn would last only 10 hours. Saturn also has the most satellites, 18 in all.

Pluto is the smallest planet. It is also the coldest and the furthest from the Sun. Its orbit is noticeably inclined. Pluto takes more than 248 Earth years to complete one orbit around the Sun.

Venus is the planet which shines brightest. This is because it is surrounded by clouds, which reflect the light of the Sun. Spinning on its axis in a clockwise direction, Venus is very hot (480°C on its surface).

Mars at around 225 million kilometres from the Sun appears red, because of the oxydization (rusting) of the metal which covers it.

Uranus has its axis on which it rotates almost parallel to the path of its orbit around the Sun. So, it orbits sideways rather than upright around the Sun. It has 15 satellites.

Earth moves around the Sun at a speed of 29.8 kilometres per second. However, it is the only planet where there is water and where life has developed.

Neptune is distinguished by a bright blue colour. Its orbit around the Sun lasts more than 164 Earth years.

49

WHAT IS THE MOON?

The Moon is Earth's only natural satellite. It is a heavenly, lifeless body which orbits around our planet, whilst accompanying Earth on its journey around the Sun. It shines in the sky because it reflects light from the Sun. Its surface is composed of volcanic rock. The Moon has no atmosphere. That is why it has been hit repeatedly by meteorites which have made numerous craters on its surface.

THE AGE OF THE MOON
It is estimated that the Moon is about 4.5 billion years old. It is widely believed that the Moon was formed from a chip of the Earth which broke away when our planet was hit by a huge heavenly body before it solidified completely.

• HOW WHY WHAT WHEN •

How is it that the Moon raises the level of the seas on Earth?

The rise and fall in the level of the sea – high and low tides – are due to the force of gravity of the Moon and to a lesser extent of the Sun. The Moon, like a huge magnet, attracts liquid masses in the Earth's hemisphere which is turned towards it, causing high tides. These happens twice each day, approximately every 12 hours and 25 minutes.

FACTS·AND·FIGURES

• On average, the Moon is 384,600km distant from the Earth. Because its orbit is elliptic, sometimes it is nearer, sometimes further from our planet.
• The Moon's diameter is a quarter of Earth's diameter – 3475.6km.
• The average temperature on the Moon goes from 100°C by day to minus 150°C by night.
• The hemisphere visible on the Moon is so vast that it could contain the whole of Europe.

THE SEAS ON THE MOON

When the Moon was first observed through telescopes, astronomers believed that the dark areas on the Moon's surface were seas. In fact, the 'seas' are vast plains of lava on the beds of gigantic meteorite craters.

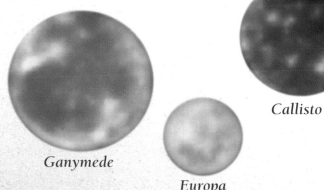

Ganymede

Callisto

Europa

Titan

Io

ARE THERE OTHER MOONS?

Planets in the Solar System have different numbers of satellites or 'moons': Mars has 2; Jupiter 16; Saturn 18; Uranus 15; Neptune 8; Pluto 1.

Jupiter's largest moons are Ganymede, Callisto, Io and Europa, all discovered in 1610 by Galileo Galilei. Scientists think there may be water in a liquid state on Europa.

Mars' two moons are very small; 16km and 18km in diameter.

One of Saturn's moons, Titan, has an atmosphere of nitrogen and methane, which may suggest the presence of elementary forms of life.

Charon, Pluto's only known moon, is half the size of the planet.

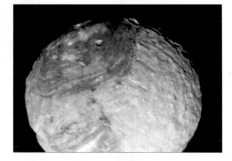

Miranda

Miranda, one of the moons of Uranus, has a very irregular surface, with plains, craters and canyons.

Triton, Neptune's largest moon, is the coldest place in the whole of the Solar System.

WHY DOES THE MOON NEVER LOOK THE SAME?

The Moon shines because it is illuminated by the Sun. It orbits around the Earth, whilst at the same time it accompanies Earth around the Sun. So, the position of the Moon in respect to our planet goes through different phases. The Moon is 'full' when it is directly opposite the Sun. It looks like a scythe when it receives light from the Sun sideways. It almost disappears when the Sun, behind it, only illuminates the side of the Moon which we never see. The phases during which the Moon is almost invisible is called the 'New Moon'. Between the New Moon and the 'Full Moon' (or 'waxing moon') there is the 'Crescent Moon'. Between the Full Moon and the New Moon is the Waning Moon.

• HOW WHY WHAT WHEN •

What is an Eclipse?

In the Solar System, planets can make shadows, one falling on another, according to their position in respect of the Sun. A solar eclipse happens when the Moon comes between the Earth and the Sun and projects a shadow on to the Sun which can hide the whole or a part. During a total eclipse, the sky darkens and only the corona of the Sun is visible, which we can see with special filters.

A lunar eclipse takes place when the Earth comes between the Moon and the Sun and the Moon passes through the shadow of the Earth. The Moon is not completely obscured, but is a pinkish colour. This is because some rays of the Sun still reach it, through the atmosphere of Earth.

THE "HUMP" OF THE MOON

There is an old saying - 'hump to the east of the Moon waning, hump to the west waxing'. This means that, to find out whether the Moon is in a waxing or waning phase, just look to see if the illuminated part has the 'hump' turned to the east or towards the west.

To understand the rotating movement of the Moon, we can use a puppet to represent the Earth, and a toy car to represent the Moon.

1) Put the puppet on a table. Take the toy car and push around the puppet. If you were in the place of the puppet, you would always see the same side of the toy car.

2) Now pick up the puppet and make the car go around it again. Watch the car, keeping your eyes at the height of the table. From this viewpoint, you can see it from all sides as it completes an entire orbit.

WHY DO WE ALWAYS SEE THE SAME SIDE OF THE MOON?

The Moon orbits in an anti-clockwise around the Earth, taking 27 days and 3 hours. Within the same interval of time it also completes a complete rotation on its own axis. That is why it is always the same side towards the Earth, making it seem that the Moon does not move. But we can try and understand the movements of the Moon as if we were looking at it from the outside.

LUNAR PHASES

The cycle of lunar phases is called a 'lunar month' and lasts about 29 and a half days.

The yellow part of the Moon indicates the side visible from Earth.
At the end of its orbit around the Earth, the Moon has completed one rotation on its own axis.

How many times has man landed on the Moon?

The US spacecraft Apollo 11 made a 'moon landing' possible. The first walk on the Moon was by Neil Armstrong and Edwin 'Buzz' Aldrin on 20 July 1969, after landing on the Moon's surface in the Lunar Module. A further five landings followed. The most recent was with Apollo 17, in December 1972. So far, twelve astronauts have explored the Moon.

THE THIRD ASTRONAUT
During the walk on the Moon by Neil Armstrong and Buzz Aldrin, a third astronaut, Michael Collins, waited in orbit around the Moon, in the Command Module.

● HOW WHY WHAT WHEN ●

Why do astronauts walk in 'bounces' on the surface of the Moon?

The weight of an object depends on the force of gravity in the place where that object is. On the Moon, the force of gravity is six times weaker than on Earth. So, the weight of a man on the Moon is one sixth that of a man on Earth. If on Earth he weighed 60kg, on the Moon he would weigh 10kg. Muscular force means he can easily overcome the weak attraction of the Moon's surface.

HOW WAS THE SPACECRAFT APOLLO II CONSTRUCTED?
Apollo II had three modules; the Service Module (SM), the Command Module (CM) and the Lunar Module (LEM). Neil Armstrong and Buzz Aldrin landed in the LEM, using the 4-legged descent stage.

Q·U·I·Z

1) During which mission did astronauts stay longest on the Moon?

❑ Apollo 13   ❑ Apollo 17   ❑ Apollo 11

2) Which sea did Apollo 11 land on?

❑ The Sea of Tranquility

❑ The Sea of Crises

❑ The Ocean of Storms

3) The first photographs of the hidden side of the Moon were taken by?

❑ Soviet Space Probe Lunik in 1959

❑ Apollo 11 in 1969

❑ Apollo 8 in 1968

4) The Lunar Module of Apollo was called?

❑ Eagle   ❑ Columbia   ❑ Lunar Prospector

Answers
1) Apollo 17, 22 hours and 5 minutes
2) In the Sea of Tranquility
3) In 1959, by the Space Probe Lunik   4) Eagle

MAN'S FOOTPRINTS

The footprints of the astronauts and the equipment they used on the Moon will remain forever, because on the Moon there is neither wind nor rain.

The descent stage of the LEM was left behind on the Moon. Together, the three modules were launched into space by the three-stage space rocket Saturn 5. After the launch, Saturn 5 detached itself and dispersed. At the end of the Space Mission, only the Command Module returned to Earth, after separating from the others.

WHO MADE THE FIRST JOURNEY INTO SPACE?

The first success in overcoming the gravity of Earth and to leave Earth's atmosphere was by Sputnik I, a Russian artificial satellite. It was launched into space by powerful rockets in 1957.

The first space exploration by a human being was in 1961. Russian astronaut Yuri Gagarin was launched into space in the space capsule Vostok I and made a complete orbit around the Earth in 1 hour and 29 minutes at an estimated speed of 28000km per hour.

THE FIRST ORBIT AROUND THE EARTH

Sputnik I made an orbit around the Earth in 1 hour and 35 minutes, transmitting some very important data regarding features of Earth's atmosphere.

THE FIRST DOG IN SPACE

Before the space flight of Gagarin, Sputnik 2 was launched with a dog, Laika, on board, in order to study the reactions of a living animal to the conditions of a flight into space.

Sputnik 2

● HOW WHY WHAT WHEN ●

Who was the first woman in space?

The Russian Valentina Tereshkova was the first lady in Space. In 1963, she journeyed for two days on board the spacecraft Vostok 6, completing 48 orbits around the Earth.

FACTS·AND·FIGURES

The stages leading to the Moon landing

• **1957-58** – launch of the first artificial satellite and the first living thing (the dog Laika) into Space.

• **1959** – the first unmanned Space Probe towards the Moon. Lunik 1, 2, 3 (ex USSR).

• **1961** – first man in Space; Yuri Gagarin (ex USSR) on board Vostok 1.

• **1962** – second man in Space: John Glenn (USA) on board spacecraft Mercury 6.

• **1962** – first Space Probe to reach the Moon: Ranger 4 (USA)

• **1965** – first man to walk in Space outside a multi-stage Space Capsule: Aleksis Leonov (ex USSR)

• **1965** – first American multi-stage Space Capsule: Gemini 3.

• **1966** – first unmanned Moon landing: Lunik 9 (ex USSR)

• **1968** – first manned spaceflight to orbit around the Moon. Apollo 8 (USA)

• **1969** – first Moon Landing by man. Apollo 11 (USA)

TO DEFEAT THE FORCE OF GRAVITY

In order to overcome the force of gravity, space vehicles need a thrust which goes in the opposite direction. Rockets are the only method capable of giving an astronaut a thrust which is sufficient to leave Earth's atmosphere.

WHICH PLANETS HAVE BEEN EXPLORED?

The only heavenly body which has been directly explored by man is the Moon. Other explorations have been made by Space Probes – without passengers, controlled from Earth, and capable of covering great distances and even reaching places far from the Solar System. The equipment on board these Space Probes give Control Stations data and images on the chemical and physical characteristics of the heavenly bodies. Some Space Probes have landed on surfaces of planets or satellites. The Russian Space Probe Venere has landed on Mars and in 1997 the Space Probe Pathfinder put the Robot Explorer Sojourner on Mars.

Other Space Probes have transmitted detailed data and images of all planets in the Solar System.

Pioneer 10

WHAT IS GRAVITATIONAL SLING-SHOT?

A Space Probe cannot carry large quantites of fuel. So, instead of using engines to change direction or to accelerate, the Probe is directed nearer a planet. The force of gravity from this planet can then control the curved path of the Probe and its speed. This operation is called 'gravitational sling-shot'.

• HOW WHY WHAT WHEN •

Can a Space Probe leave the Solar System

The US Space Probe Pioneer 10 was launched in 1972. After having gone beyond the orbit of Neptune, it is now directed towards Proxima Centurai, towards at the edge of the Solar System. Proxima Centurai is the star nearest to us. Pioneer 10 will reach it in about 26,000 years. Pioneer 10 was overtaken in 1998 by the Space Probe Voyager 1, after having gone near Saturn. Voyager 1 is now the Space Probe furthest from Earth – at a distance of 0.4 billion kilometres!

Is it possible to live on the Moon?

Living on the Moon would mean that we could use the resources of its sub-surface, rich in metals, to build scientific laboratories, launch-bases and space observatories. The project to populate the Moon may provide solutions to enable the growth of food, electrical energy to provide protection from solar radiation and extremes of temperature and to remedy the lack of gravity. But the biggest problem will be the total lack of water. However, in 1996, the US Lunar Space Probe Clementine sent back information that both poles of the Moon are covered with a great mass of water in its solid state, confirmed two years later by the US Lunar Robot Prospector. This discovery has re-opened the door to the possibility of a lunar city.

What will a lunar city be like?

It will have solar panels for the production of electrical energy, laboratories, shops, and areas for the landing and take-off of space vehicles. One of the projects forecast for the Lunar City (Escargot City 2050) are houses and buildings similar to the shells of snails. (*Escargot* is French for snail.)

A JOURNEY INTO SPACE

The special spacesuit which astronauts wear for their 'walks in space' enable them to breathe oxygen, to overcome the extremely cold temperatures of Outer Space and also to carry out, in the absence of gravity, repairs to the spacecraft or to the space base. To protect the astronaut from cold the spacesuit inside is criss-crossed with little tubes containing hot liquid, like little radiators to give warmth to the smallest finger. When necessary, the astronaut can also put on the spacesuit inside the spacecraft to refresh himself with oxygen. On the front of the spacesuit is the housing for all tools, each with a retractable thread so that nothing floats off into space. The helmet is fixed to the spacesuit and inside the astronaut can turn his head freely. The visor is mirrored, to protect the eyes from solar radiation.

When the astronaut has to work on the remote-control arms, he has to stay firmly in a particular place. So, he puts his feet into special boots fixed to the walls.

- The spacesuit worn for 'walks in space' weighs 47kg.
- The helmet weighs 4kg.
- There are buttons for the propulsion of the MMU (Manoeuvre Movement Unit).
- The remote-controlled robot arm which is controlled from inside the Shuttle can launch and retrieve satellites in space. It can also carry out repairs. It is divided into three parts and can be moved in six directions. Each arm is 16.8m long.
- The EMU (Extra-vehicular Mobility Unit) weighs 68kg and contains batteries, cooling systems and oxygen.

HOW DOES AN ASTRONAUT MOVE IN SPACE?

Thanks to the MMU the astronaut can move on a sort of flying armchair. This has push-buttons on the arms to manoeuvre the movement.

The EMU comes fixed to the back and is equipped with a little rocket which the astronaut uses to move.

HOW IS A SPACECRAFT SET OUT?

The 1970 Space Mission was carried out using non-reusable vehicles, which were mostly destroyed. The Space Shuttle vehicles have been designed to use many times and have been designed to transport and to put into orbit artificial satellites or to transport laboratories and space stations.

The Shuttle comprises a vehicle similar to an aeroplane, the Orbiter, which enters in orbit and then returns to Earth by two outer recoverable rockets, called 'boosters', and by one giant external fuel tank. The Shuttle is equipped with manoeuvrable motors to control the flight both in orbit and the return.

- The hold of the Space Shuttle is 18m long and 4m wide.
- The Shuttle can carry in orbit 29 tonnes of cargo and bring back 15 tonnes to Earth.
- In 1986 the Space Shuttle Challenger on its tenth flight exploded soon after its launch, killing seven members of the crew; launches were suspended for two years after.
- In 1988 the ex Soviet Union launched their first unmanned space shuttle, Buran.

THE PHASES OF FLIGHT

1) Launch is vertical, pushed up by the principal motors and booster rockets.

2) At a height of around 50km, the booster drops off and falls into the ocean.

3) At 100km, the external fuel tank drops off and disintegrates in the atmosphere.

4) With the aid of the manoeuvre motor, the spacecraft goes into orbit and reaches maximum speed.

5) To come back, the spacecraft positions itself in the opposite direction and fires the motors to move out of orbit.

6) At re-entry into the atmosphere, the spacecraft overheats by friction with the air and at some points reaches about 1500°C.

7) Finally the Shuttle lands in a gliding flight and comes down with the aid of a parachute.

IS IT POSSIBLE TO LIVE IN SPACE?

For some years, the USA, Russia, Europe, Canada and Japan have been working on the construction of the largest Space Station ever realized. It is hoped that this will come into use some time during the first years of the 21st Century. Inside there will be six laboratories, in which scientists from all over the world will work together. Both the equipment and the scientists will undergo a rigorous training programme, under the constant control of doctors during their time in space, which could last more than three or four months. As before, the main challenge to human beings will be to adapt themselves to the lack of gravity, being able to work, to wash, to eat and to sleep in Space in the same way as they do on Earth.

● HOW WHY WHAT WHEN ●

What other space stations have been launched in space?

The first Russian Space Station Salyut ('Salute') 1 was put into orbit in 1971. The last was Salyut 7 in 1982. Skylab was launched in 1973 by the USA. The last crew returned to Earth in 1974. In 1979, the Station disintegrated into the atmosphere. The Russian Space Station Mir was in service from 1986 to 1997.

THE BODY IN SPACE

Tests and studies on astronauts have shown that, during space missions, the muscles become weakened and the bones lose calcium.

HOW DO PEOPLE LIVE IN A SPACE STATION?

Inside the Space Station all is arranged to overcome the lack of gravity. In the shower-rooms, the water is sucked up from the floor to avoid it flying away! In the laboratories, there are hooks to keep boots firmly fixed, so that scientists can

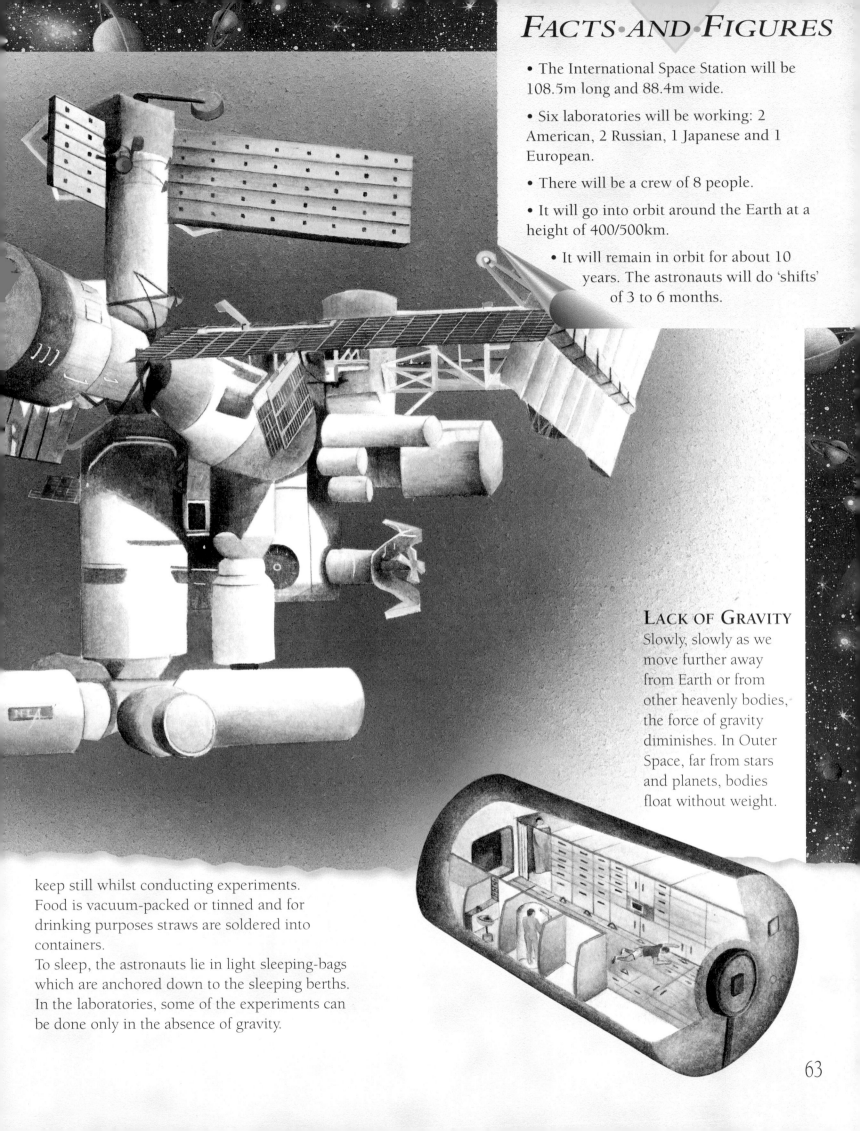

FACTS·AND·FIGURES

- The International Space Station will be 108.5m long and 88.4m wide.

- Six laboratories will be working: 2 American, 2 Russian, 1 Japanese and 1 European.

- There will be a crew of 8 people.

- It will go into orbit around the Earth at a height of 400/500km.

- It will remain in orbit for about 10 years. The astronauts will do 'shifts' of 3 to 6 months.

LACK OF GRAVITY
Slowly, slowly as we move further away from Earth or from other heavenly bodies, the force of gravity diminishes. In Outer Space, far from stars and planets, bodies float without weight.

keep still whilst conducting experiments. Food is vacuum-packed or tinned and for drinking purposes straws are soldered into containers.
To sleep, the astronauts lie in light sleeping-bags which are anchored down to the sleeping berths. In the laboratories, some of the experiments can be done only in the absence of gravity.

63

WHAT DOES AN ARTIFICIAL SATELLITE DO?

The sky above us is full of numerous artificial satellites, put into orbit around the Earth for many purposes – to receive and transmit television and telephonic signals, to relay data on weather conditions, to observe regions of the planet for military, industrial and agricultural purposes, furnishing data for study on Earth about pollution, mapping the stars and to keep track of the navigation of ships and aircraft. Artificial satellites are often equipped with solar panels which transform the rays of the Sun into an energy which can be used in their work.

HOW DO ARTIFICIAL SATELLITES REMAIN IN ORBIT?

When an object is launched into the air, it makes a curved trail. To prevent space vehicles falling back to Earth, they need rockets to give them a speed of at least 27000km per hour. In this way, the vehicle overcomes the force of gravity, finishes its launching stage and enters into orbit around the Earth, always travelling at the same distance, just like natural satellites.

Dinosaurs

WHEN DID DINOSAURS LIVE?

Dinosaurs first appeared on Earth about 225 million years ago - when our planet was already thousands of millions of years old and the continents as we know them were joined together in one huge land mass. Dinosaurs were reptiles. One of the earliest-known species, the arcosaurs, were like crocodiles, with strong hind legs and a long tail. Dinosaurs dominated the Earth for 160 million years. They existed until the end of the Cretaceous Era, about 65 million years ago.

ORIGIN OF THE NAME

The name dinosaur comes from the Greek word *deinos* meaning 'terrible' and *saurus* meaning 'lizard'.

LIFE ON EARTH

According to scientists, Earth is about 4.5 billion years old. The earliest form of life developed only after 1.5 billion years - about 3 billion years ago.

Rutiodon

• HOW WHEN WHAT WHY •

How are dinosaurs divided into groups?

Dinosaurs can be divided into two groups according to the shape of the pelvis. The saurischia (lizard-hipped) dinosaurs had a pelvis like a lizard, with the bottom hip bones spread out, and the ornithischia, or bird-hipped dinosaurs, had the bottom hip bones close together. The saurischia included some herbivores (plant-eaters) and all the carnivores (meat-eaters). The ornithischia were all herbivores.

ARCOSAURS AND CROCODILES

Crocodiles are the only survivors of the arcosaur group. They differ from arcosaurs mainly by their nostrils, which are at the very end of the nose, and not so close to the eyes as those of the arcosaur.

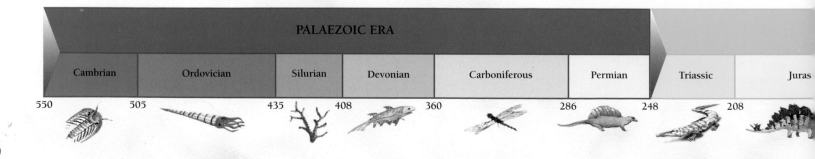

PALAEZOIC ERA							
Cambrian	Ordovician	Silurian	Devonian	Carboniferous	Permian	Triassic	Juras
550	505	435	408	360	286	248	208

1) What were the first living things on Earth?
❐ reptiles   ❐ jellyfish and seaweed   ❐ fish

2) Dinosaurs appeared during which era –
❐ Mesozoic   ❐ Palaeozoic   ❐ Cainozoic

3) What class of animal was the dinosaur?
❐ reptile   ❐ mammal   ❐ amphibian

4) In which period did dinosaurs become extinct?
❐ Triassic   ❐ Jurassic   ❐ Cretaceous

Answers
1) jellyfish and seaweed 2) Mesozoic
3) reptile 4) Cretaceous

Cryolophosaurus

DINOSAURS AND REPTILES

What made dinosaurs different from other reptiles was the position of their hind legs; instead of moving first on one side and then the other, like crocodiles and lizards, a dinosaur moved 'wagging its tail' – the hind limbs of a dinosaur were quite straight under its body, so that it could walk and run in an upright position.

THE LONG STORY OF EARTH

• The story of the Earth can be divided into eras, with each era sub-divided into periods.
• In the Palaeozoic Era there was already a wide range of living things.
• The Mesozoic Era was the time when dinosaurs began to live on Earth. This era can be sub-divided into three periods - the Triassic, the Jurassic and the Cretaceous.
• The Cainozoic Era was the time when the human race began.

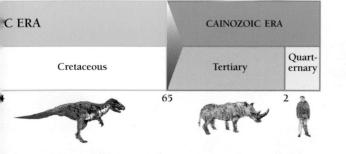

C ERA	CAINOZOIC ERA		
Cretaceous	Tertiary	Quart-ernary
	65		2

67

WHAT DID THE EARTH LOOK LIKE IN THE TRIASSIC PERIOD?

By the end of the Triassic Period, dinosaurs had just appeared. The climate was hot and dry, the deserts more and more extensive. Vast, humid areas to either side of rivers and along the coasts of the oceans were covered with ferns and plants such as horsetails. Inland there grew forests of Conifers, Ginkgo trees and Palms. Because of the climate, the gigantic amphibians had disappeared. But the reptiles were able to survive, as did the invertebrates (insects, crustaceans, molluscs), on which the reptiles could feed. And from these early reptiles, the first mammals developed.

The *Kuehneosaurus* was a reptile which glided from one branch to another, hunting for insects.

Kuehneosaurus

Pterosaur

THE BEGINNINGS

The thecodonts were the most common reptiles, outnumbering all others. From thecodonts originated pterosaurs (flying reptiles, from the Greek *pterón,* meaning 'wing'), dinosaurs and crocodiles.

• HOW WHEN WHY •

Did birds exist in the Triassic period?

In the Triassic Period, the only flying creatures (other than insects) were pterosaurs, the flying reptiles. The first true bird, the Archaeopterix, appeared during the next period, the Jurassic Period, with numerous other species appearing during the Cretaceous Period.

The first mammals were about 10 centimetres long; as protection against enemies, a mammal hunted only during the night. The *Protosuchus,* ancestor of today's crocodile, lived almost completely on land.

Protosuchus

FACTS·AND·FIGURES

- Conifers in the Triassic Period were over 30m.
- Amphibians (creatures living on land, but laying their eggs in water, such as frogs and newts) were huge in Triassic times, compared to today. The Micropholis, for example, looked like a salamander and was about 20cm long.
- One of the first mammals, the Morganucodon, was only 10cm long.

Pangea

JUST ONE CONTINENT

In the Triassic Period, more than 200 million years ago, all the land was joined together to form one continent, called the Pangea. So animals could migrate from one area to another.

Plateosaurus

Coelophysis

WHICH WERE THE FIRST DINOSAURS?

The *Plateosaurus* was a plant-eating dinosaur with a long, thin neck. With a length of 10m, it was one of the largest of its time. On its front limbs it had big claws which it could use both to pull down the highest branches and defend itself from enemies.

The *Procompsognatus* was about the same size as a turkey. It could run very quickly and fed on insects, lizards and mammals.

The *Coelophysis* was a meat-eating dinosaur, light and agile and about 3m long. It was probably a cannibal, feeding on the young of its own species.

The *Saltopus* was only 60cm in length. It was one of the smallest meat-eating dinosaurs that ever existed.

WHAT ARE FOSSILS?

How can we prove that dinosaurs existed? The answer is found in fossils, the remains of plants and animals which lived millions of years ago and preserved in rock. Bodies of animals, mollusc shells, egg-shells, remains of plants... all these became encased by layers of mud and sand. Over millions of years, these layers became solidified until they formed rocks, and this process also transformed the plant and animal remains into rock. Some fossils were preserved in ice, in tar and in amber (a fossilized form of sticky resin which oozed from trees). By studying fossils, scientists have reconstructed the story of the Earth, how it changed and developed, its geography and the different forms of animal and plant-life which have now disappeared. From fossilized bones, we can discover the shapes and sizes of dinosaurs; from their teeth, their diet; and from footprints, the walk and the speed of these prehistoric animals.

● HOW WHEN WHAT WHY ●

Was it only bones that were fossilized?

No. The prints of some parts of the body of an animal - footprints, for example, or scales from the skin - might also be fossilized. From these prints, we can discover the shape and size of a bone or part of the body. The whole fossil is soaked in chemicals to dissolve the rock, until only the impression of the print is left. This hole can then be filled with plaster, to produce a cast.

A PALAEONTOLOGIST

A palaeontologist is a scientist who studies the fossils of animal and plant life, in order to re-construct their shape, the structure of their organs, their behaviour and discover the reasons why they died out or developed.

HOW DID A FOSSIL BEGIN?

When a jungle animal dies, its body is eaten by hyenas, jackals and vultures, then beetles and worms decompose the body. The Sun, rain and frost wears away the skeleton, and in time it becomes part of the soil. Much the same would have happened to dinosaurs and prehistoric mammals.

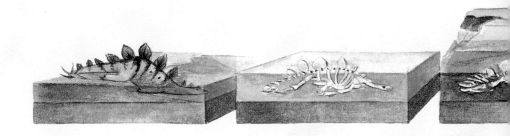

FACTS·AND·FIGURES

- At the end of the 17th century, two gigantic jaws were discovered in Holland. These belonged to a marine reptile of the Mesozoic Era, the Mosasaurus.
- The first discovery of the head an Ichthyosaur, a sea reptile, was by an 11-year old girl, Mary Anning, at the beginning of the 18th century.
- In 1882, the discovery of a gigantic tooth, similar to that of an iguana, proved the theory of the existence of a gigantic, extinct reptile, the Iguanodon.
- In 1878, in Belgium, 30 skeletons of adult Iguanodons were found, almost all of them complete.
- Between 1877 and 1890, 126 species of dinosaur were identified. More than 500 species have been identified to date.

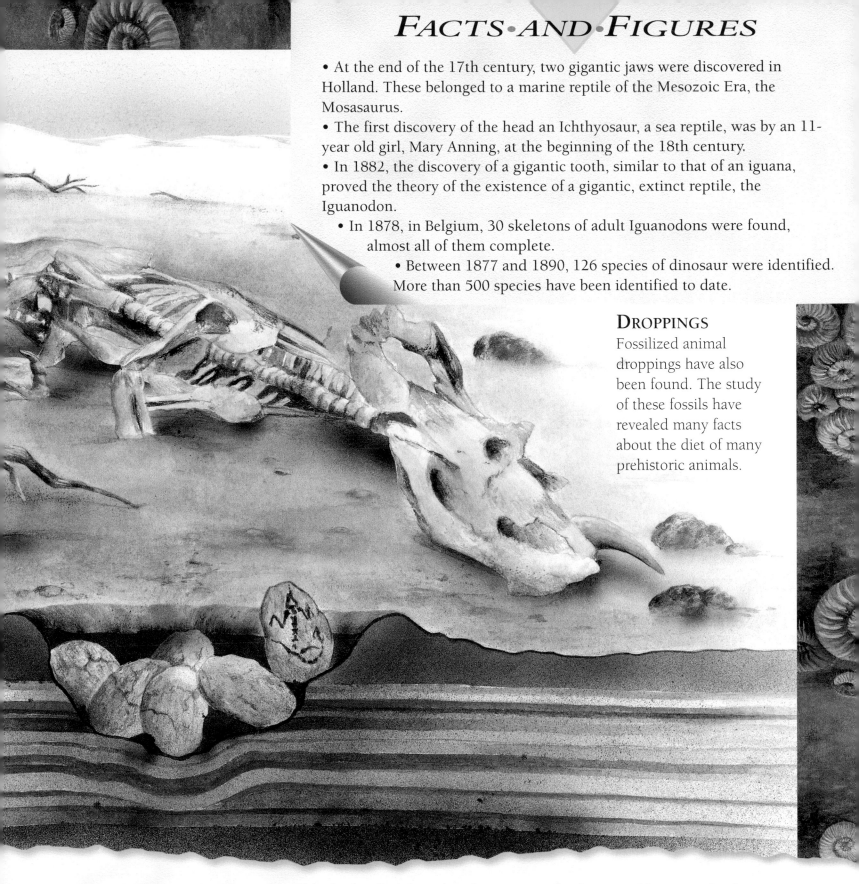

DROPPINGS

Fossilized animal droppings have also been found. The study of these fossils have revealed many facts about the diet of many prehistoric animals.

But if the body of an animal sank to the sea bed, or the bottom of a lake or swamp, it became buried in the mud, sand, or the cinders of a volcano. Over the course of millions of years, the animal's skeleton, sealed off from the air, became transformed into rock.

This happened by mineral substances filling the porous parts (spaces with channels or tubes) of the skeleton, or by taking the place of the original material, turning the bones into stone. Millions of years later, through movements of the Earth's Crust or erosion, fossils come to the surface.

71

WERE ALL DINOSAURS ENORMOUS?

Not all dinosaurs were gigantic. In fact, the first dinosaurs were quite small, not more than 4 - 5 metres in length. But gradually, they developed into different species. Some reached an enormous size, in height as well as length. Others were rather small, some only as big as present-day hens. The sauropods, a group of plant-eaters which included the Brachiosaurus, Apatosaurus and Diplodocus were the longest, the tallest and the heaviest dinosaurs that ever lived. They had long necks and tails, with a small head, and were ten times bigger than an elephant.

The neck of the *Diplodocus* was more than 7m long. This dinosaur could grow to a length of more than 27m - as long as seven cars parked end to end!

• HOW WHEN WHAT WHY •

How were dinosaurs named?

Some names describe the appearance of a dinosaur, or a particular feature. Others are named after the place where their remains were discovered, or the name of the person who discovered them.

Here are some examples:

Albertosaurus - 'Alberta lizard', named after the Canadian province of Alberta, where its remains were first discovered.

Maiasaura - 'good mother lizard'. It is believed that this dinosaur took particularly good care of its young.

Arctosaurus - ' Arctic lizard' - the remains of this dinosaur were found in the Arctic Circle.

Fulgurotherium - 'thunderbolt animal'. This dinosaur is thought to have been a very fast runner!

Deinonychus - 'terrible claw'. It had a dangerous, single claw at the end of the second toe on its hind legs.

WHICH WERE THE SMALLEST DINOSAURS?

One of the smallest dinosaurs was the *Compsognathus*, an agile and alert hunter, which did not grow more than 80cm long and weighed only about 3kg. Its front legs had three small, sharp claws.

The *Brachiosaurus* was more than 10m in height (which means it would have been able to look over the top of a three storey house). It was also 23m long, more than a railway container wagon.

- One of the largest dinosaurs in the Theropod (meat-eating) group was the *Tyrannosaurus Rex*.

- Despite its enormous size, the *Diplodocus* had the smallest brain of all dinosaurs.

- The *Mamenchisaurus* could boast the longest neck - 11m long!

- The longest tail (up to 11m long) belonged to the *Diplodocus*.

Compsognathus

The *Lesothosaurus*, a light and quick-moving plant-eater, only grew to about one metre in length. It was as big as the average dog, with slender rear legs and very short front legs.

Lesothosaurus

HOW DID DINOSAURS MOVE?

Slow or fast, on two or four legs... dinosaurs walked and moved in many different ways which scientists are able to establish by examining the prints of fossils and bones of the limbs. The long tibia (shinbone) and the muscular thigh of the Velociraptor, or the long tapering legs of the Gallimimus, for example, indicate a two-legged movement. They were able to run when needed, and, like the powerful Tyrannosaurus Rex and Allosaurus, with their long and strong hind legs, they could run short distances very fast indeed. An enormous sauropod or ceratops like the Triceratops, moved very slowly, on four heavy legs and huge feet, which gave solid support for its massive, heavy body.

SOME COULD CLIMB...
Some scientists believe that the most agile dinosaurs were also able to climb trees.

Brachiosaurus

Tuojiangosaurus

● HOW WHEN WHAT WHY ●

How did dinosaurs use their tails?

The long tails of many dinosaurs were very useful to them, to keep their balance as they ran, or if they needed to stand on their hind legs.

It seems that the muscular tail of the *Iguanodon* supported the body, like the tail of a kangaroo.

The *Deinonychus*, that fast and fearsome hunter, could keep its tail outstretched behind, using it as a rudder to keep its direction in a zig-zag run.

The plant-eaters used the tail according to its shape – as a whip, or as a cudgel – to defend itself against enemies.

FACTS·AND·FIGURES

- The *Dromiceiomimus* was one of the fastest dinosaurs, reaching speeds of about 65km per hour.
- The *Gallimimus* looked rather like an ostrich. It is thought to have reached 56km per hour, the same speed as a galloping horse.
- The *Struthiomimus* could run at about 50km per hour.
- The *Brachiosaurus* was probably the slowest dinosaur, moving no faster than 4 - 6km per hour!
- The actual 'speed record' for a land animal today is held by the cheetah. Even over short distances, it can reach 96km per hour.

Gallimimus

...SOME COULD RUN

Running was the only defence for the smaller plant-eaters, who had to flee from predators (animals who hunted them as prey).

Dromiceiomimus

WERE THERE MARINE DINOSAURS?

The gigantic *Plesiosaurs* and *Ichthyosaurs* were not dinosaurs, but sea reptiles. They dominated the sea for the whole of the Jurassic and the Cretaceous Period.

Ichthyosaurs were very fast swimmers and looked rather like dolphins. They had a tapered body, a thick tail and front limbs very similar to oars. Numerous fossilized remains have shown that, like dolphins, they gave birth to living young. *Plesiosaurs* generally had long necks, small heads and long fins for swimming.

75

WERE THERE FLYING DINOSAURS?

All dinosaurs lived on land, and none could fly. However, at the end of the Triassic Period, there appeared the pterosaurs, flying reptiles, from the same family as dinosaurs. The name means 'flying lizard'. The front limbs of a pterosaur ended in three clawed fingers, plus a fourth, very long, finger which supported the wing - a light membrane of skin joined to the side of the body. Some pterosaurs also used these limbs to move about on land.

EXTINCTION

It is estimated that there were about 120 species of pterosaurs. They became extinct at the same time as the dinosaurs.

Pterodactylus

● HOW WHEN WHAT WHY ●

What were pterodactyls?

Pterodactyls ('wing finger') belonged to the pterosaur group, but they appeared much later. They were quite large in size, with a long tail and skull and a long neck.

THE TAIL

A pterosaur had a flexible (easily bent) tail, which it could use as a whip.

FACTS·AND·FIGURES

• The largest pterosaurs were the *Quetzalcoatlus* and the *Ornithocheirus*. Both had a wing span of about 12 metres.

• The smallest was the *Batrachognathus,* which was about the same size as a raven.

• The *Pteranodon* ('with wings, without teeth') had a wing span of 7 metres and a body as large as a turkey.

Dimorphodon

WHAT DID PTEROSAURS FEED ON?

By examining the structure of jaws and beaks, scientists have been able to determine the diet of the pterosaur. For instance, the *Dimophodon* had two types of teeth - pointed teeth at the front of the beak, smaller teeth at the back, with which it could catch insects in the air and on the ground.

The *Pterodactylus* had long, narrow jaws. Its sharp teeth were ideal for seizing and holding slippery prey, such as fish or worms.

The *Pterodaustro* fed on small sea creatures. Its narrow teeth in the bottom jaw acted as a sieve, letting out water and trapping the food inside. It would then chew its prey with the smaller teeth in the upper jaw.

The *Dzungaripterus* had jaws as strong as pincers, perfect for crushing the shells of molluscs.

udimorphodon

Pterodaustro

A LIGHTWEIGHT SKELETON

The skeleton of the pterosaur was ideal for flying because it was very light. All the bones were thin, most hollow. Despite this, scientists doubt that pterosaurs could actually fly up from the ground - they probably launched themselves into flight from cliffs or trees.

Scaphognathus

HOW WERE BABY DINOSAURS BORN?

Baby dinosaurs hatched from eggs. But, unlike other reptiles, dinosaurs did not leave their eggs after they were laid. Instead, they sat on them and looked after their young. The study of fossils has led to the discovery of dinosaur 'nurseries', where some dinosaurs would return each year in a group to lay their eggs and rear their young. The nests were built close together, so that they could be defended against enemies more easily. Some nests were covered with sand and leaves, probably to keep the eggs warm whilst the parents went in search of food. The egg of a dinosaur was quite small compared to the size of the adult. For example, the egg of a hadrosaur (duck-billed dinosaur) was only as large as a man's hand.

A CRATER OF MUD
A hadrosaur (a dinosaur with a beak like a duck's bill) built its nests of mud, raised up from the ground. Each was about 2m wide and 1m deep, like a crater of mud.

• HOW WHEN WHAT WHY •

Which animals today hatch their young in groups?

Gulls, albatross and penguins hatch their young in groups. They build nests with a span which is equal to the size of the adult bird. This means that the space taken up by the nest can be covered by the adult body. Also, nests are in a group and so can be kept under the control of a few adult birds whilst the others go in search of food.

1) *How large do you think the largest dinosaur egg ever found was?*
☐ 30 cm   ☐ 15 cm   ☐ 1 m

2) *What is the largest number of dinosaur eggs found in the same place?*
☐ 10   ☐ 5   ☐ 30

3) *What do you think the shell of a dinosaur egg was like?*
☐ rough and thick
☐ hard and tough
☐ thin

Answers
1) 30 cm 2) 30
3) hard and tough

WHAT WERE BABY DINOSAURS LIKE?

Baby dinosaurs were about 30cm long when they hatched. They were unable to look after themselves and were fed in the nest until they were fully mature. The discovery of fossilized skeletons of many sizes tell us that animals of different ages - new-born, young and adult - lived together in the same group.

HOLES IN THE SAND

The *Protoceratops* laid its eggs in holes dug out of sand; the nest was set out in concentric circles (circles with a common centre), rising up from the ground.

During migration, sauropods protected their young by keeping them at the centre of the herd, like many other plant-eaters did. This is borne out by many fossilized footprints.

WHAT DID DINOSAURS EAT?

Many dinosaurs ate plants, others hunted and ate living animals. Others, like jackals and vultures today, fed on the carcasses of dead animals. The numerous plant-eaters did not have to migrate, because they could get their food at different levels of the ground. The stegosaurs, with their delicate teeth, or the ceratops, which were not very tall, fed on low bushes and shrubs. Hadrosaurs, iguanodons and sauropods could pull leaves from the tallest trees, thanks to their long necks, or by standing on their hind legs. Many meat-eaters stayed in the same areas because they had learned to attack particular types of plant-eaters.

OMNIVORES
Omnivores were dinosaurs which fed on lizards, frogs and small mammals, as well as leaves and fruit.

THE DIGESTION OF THE PLANT-EATERS
The gigantic plant-eaters with their long necks had a complex digestive system and a stomach which could grind up plant-matter.

● HOW WHEN WHAT WHY ●

Is it true that some plant-eaters ate stones?

Just as many birds today swallow grit, some plant-eaters swallowed small pebbles. These pebbles helped to grind up food in the stomach.

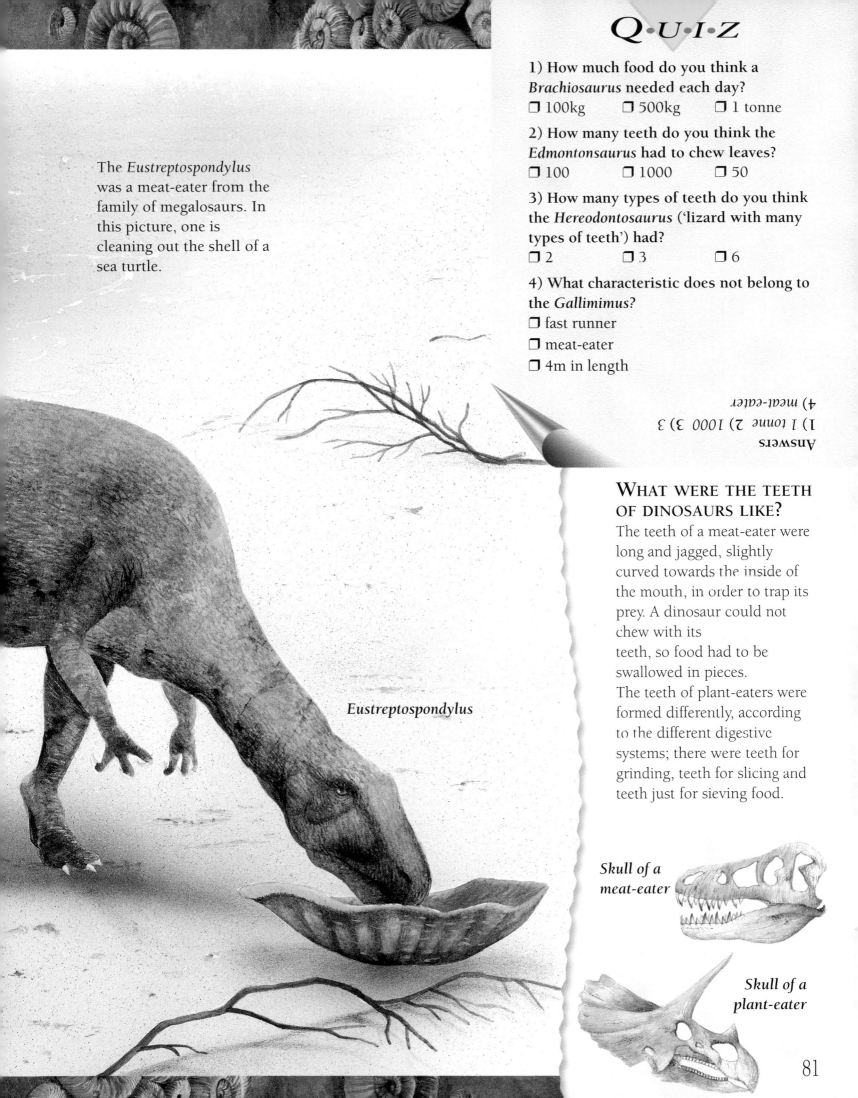

The *Eustreptospondylus* was a meat-eater from the family of megalosaurs. In this picture, one is cleaning out the shell of a sea turtle.

Eustreptospondylus

Q·U·I·Z

1) How much food do you think a *Brachiosaurus* needed each day?
❏ 100kg   ❏ 500kg   ❏ 1 tonne

2) How many teeth do you think the *Edmontonsaurus* had to chew leaves?
❏ 100   ❏ 1000   ❏ 50

3) How many types of teeth do you think the *Hereodontosaurus* ('lizard with many types of teeth') had?
❏ 2   ❏ 3   ❏ 6

4) What characteristic does not belong to the *Gallimimus*?
❏ fast runner
❏ meat-eater
❏ 4m in length

Answers
1) 1 tonne 2) 1000 3) 3
4) meat-eater

WHAT WERE THE TEETH OF DINOSAURS LIKE?

The teeth of a meat-eater were long and jagged, slightly curved towards the inside of the mouth, in order to trap its prey. A dinosaur could not chew with its teeth, so food had to be swallowed in pieces.

The teeth of plant-eaters were formed differently, according to the different digestive systems; there were teeth for grinding, teeth for slicing and teeth just for sieving food.

Skull of a meat-eater

Skull of a plant-eater

81

HOW DID THE EARTH CHANGE IN THE JURASSIC PERIOD?

In the Jurassic Period, the hot climate became more damp and humid, with increased rainfall. The Earth was covered with thick vegetation - ferns, conifers, horsetails, cycads (plants similar to palms) and Gingko Trees. Plant-eating and meat-eating dinosaurs began changing in shape and in size, occupying the whole of the Earth. Some reptiles dominated the water and the air. In the sea lived the plesiosaurs and ichthyosaurs and in the skies flew pterosaurs, becoming larger and larger. The bird appeared for the first time, with the Archaeopteryx. There were still only a few types of amphibian, and mammals came out from the undergrowth only at night to avoid predators.

Euoplocephalus

● HOW WHEN WHAT WHY ●

When did the 'armour-plated' dinosaur live?

There are two groups of 'armour-plated' dinosaurs – nodosaurs, which lived during the Jurassic Period, and the ankylosaurs, which began to spread in the Cretaceous Period.
The nodosaurs were plant-eaters and rather like enormous crocodiles. They had a bony armour which covered the body, their short limbs and long tail sticking out - an appearance sure to discourage even the fiercest of meat-eaters!

TWO CONTINENTS

In the course of the Jurassic Period, the Pangea divided into two parts - Laurasia, north and Gondwana, south.

FACTS·AND·FIGURES

- The Jurassic Period, the second period of the Mesozoic Era, lasted about 60 million years.

- The plesiosaurs, sea reptiles, had long necks. The neck of the *Elasmosaurus* was 13m long.

- The *Metriorhynchus*, a sea crocodile, was a predator which grew to about 3m in length.

- Gingko Trees grew up to 30m high - the height of a 10-storey building.

INSECTS

Many of the insects that we know today, such as flies, grasshoppers and termites, first appeared in the Jurassic Period.

Archaeopteryx

THE FIRST BIRD

The *Archaeopteryx* was the first bird to appear on Earth. It looked rather like a dinosaur, with four legs with claws, a long bony tail and teeth in its beak. But its body was covered with feathers, like birds of today. It was about the size of a dove and fed on insects. Some scientists believe the *Archaeopteryx* could not fly, but fluttered about. Others think it climbed trees and then launched itself into flight by gliding.

WHY DID STEGOSAURS HAVE DORSAL PLATES?

Stegosaurs, a group of huge and peaceful plant-eating dinosaurs, were characterized by a double line of triangular plates along its back. According to some scientists, these plates regulated the body temperature of the stegosaur. By attracting the rays of the Sun, the plates would increase the body temperature. And if the stegosaur's body became too hot, the plates could disperse the heat by a short spell in the shade, or facing away from the Sun.

WHAT IS THE MEANING OF *STEGOSAURUS*?

The name *Stegosaurus* means 'roof lizard' because paleantologists believe that its dorsal plates were arranged rather like the tiles of a roof, slightly sloping and on top of the body. If, as they think, the dorsal plates were vertical and in double file, this would have made the plates perfect for regulating the body temperature.

WHAT DID THE *STEGOSAURUS* LOOK LIKE?

The *Stegosaurus* had a small head and a massive body. Its teeth were weak and therefore it is believed that it grazed on the most tender of vegetable matter.

Dorsal plates

Its powerful tail ended with spikes up to 1m long, which the *Stegosaurus* used to defend itself.
Its dorsal plates were up to 70cm high. With an average length of 9m, the *Stegosaurus* was one of the largest in the stegosaur group.

WHY DID THE CERATOPS HAVE HORNS?

The name 'ceratops' means 'horned muzzle'. In fact, this four-legged plant-eater had horns of different shapes and sizes, positioned above the eyes and at the top of the muzzle. The ceratops used these fearsome forms of defence to pierce the flesh of enemies during a fight - that is, unless the enemy was not scared off by its frightening appearance! Male ceratops also used their horns to fight other males of the same herd to decide who would be the chief, or which one would mate with a female.

● HOW WHEN WHAT WHY ●

Did the ceratops have a beak?

Another characteristic of this plant-eater was a beak, similar to the beak of a parrot. It was as strong as a pair of shears. With its beak, a ceratops could pierce the hardest root or strongest tree-bark.

WHAT WERE THE COLLARS OF CERATOPS LIKE?

The collar, or neck frill of a ceratops was made of bone covered with skin. It protected the animal from bites and from the claws of enemies.

The enormous collar of the *Chasmosaurus* covered its neck and shoulders. The male's collar could probably assume gaudy colours to attract females.

The *Pentaceratops* ('five-horned muzzle') had a collar edged with small spines.

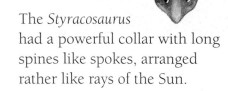

The *Styracosaurus* had a powerful collar with long spines like spokes, arranged rather like rays of the Sun.

WHAT WAS THE EARTH LIKE IN THE CRETACEOUS PERIOD?

In the Cretaceous Period, which began 146 million years ago and ended 80 million years later, the continental land-masses were much the same as they are today. Compared to the Jurassic Period, the climate was more temperate and the seasons more different. In this age there appeared the first plants with flowers, whilst grass, bushes and deciduous trees such as those we know today (oak, beech, maple) took the place of horsetail and cycad.
Among the mammals, marsupials such as the opossum made their first appearance, feeding on the pollinating insects and birds. Dinosaurs had reached the highest level of their evolution, before their extinction.

● HOW WHEN WHAT WHY ●

Why did plants with flowers appear in the Cretaceous Period?

With the presence of insects and birds to carry the pollen, plants with flowers (angiospermae) became widespread, whilst plant-eaters, such as the *Triceratops*, continued undisturbed to eat other vegetation.

Triceratops
- Height: 3 metres
- Length: 0 metres
- Weight: 10 tonnes
- Length of skull: more than 2 metres

WHEN DID THE TRICERATOPS LIVE?

The *Triceratops* ('three-horned muzzle') lived in the Cretaceous Period, 65-70 million years ago. Four massive legs supported a heavy, muscular body which was protected by a hard, thick skin. The enormous head with its three horns, ended in a powerful bony collar. The *Triceratops* was a peaceful plant-eater, but when attacked, it could use its horn to pierce its enemy.

PARROT BEAK

Being a plant-eater, the *Triceratops* could use its characteristic parrot's beak to tear and to rip apart shoots, twigs and leaves, which it would then grind up with the teeth at the back of its mouth.

WHY WAS THE TYRANNOSAURUS CALLED 'REX'?

The Tyrannosaurus Rex (king of tyrant reptiles) was the largest of all tyrannosaurs, the powerful dinosaurs of the Cretaceous Period and one of the fiercest of all predators. The Tyrannosaurus Rex had a powerful head supported by a short, strong neck. Its enormous hind legs, higher than a man, had four strong toes with powerful claws.

The front legs were very short, with two 'fingers' with sharp, pointed claws.

The Tyrannosaurus Rex walked upright, balancing its body with the aid of its powerful tail, and it could reach its prey in a few strides. But its most powerful weapon was its fearsome teeth, sharp, jagged and curved, from which no victim escaped.

● HOW WHEN WHAT WHY ●

When was a Tyrannosaurus Rex discovered?

The first complete skeleton of a *Tyrannosaurus Rex* was found in the USA in 1902. The palaeontologist H.F. Osborn studied these remains, together with others unearthed soon after and reconstructed for the first time the terrifying form of this gigantic dinosaur. In 1924 more 'three-toed' footprints were discovered from which palaeontologists calculated a stride of 4 metres. Some years later, this stride was attributed to the *Tyrannosaurus Rex*.

RELATIVES OF THE TYRANNOSAURUS REX

The *Albertosaurus* was a fierce predator which killed its victims by biting the neck. Smaller but perhaps even fiercer than the *Tyrannosaurus Rex*, it would suddenly jump on plant-eaters as they grazed.

FACTS·AND·FIGURES

Tyrannosaurus Rex
- Height: 5-6 metres
- Length: up to 12 metres
- Weight: 6 tonnes (more than an elephant)
  - Length of the head: 1 or 2 metres
    - Length of stride: about 4 metres

HEAVY BUT AGILE

The body structure of the *Tyrannosaurus Rex* was able to support its enormous weight, as well as making this dinosaur very quick and agile. Its internal organs were protected by many pairs of ribs.

METHOD OF HUNTING

According to many scientists, the *Tyrannosaurus Rex* hunted in groups (including, perhaps, the females) rather than hunting alone, attacking whole herds of plant-eaters.

Alioramus

The *Alioramus* had a long, narrow head with a series of bony lumps on its muzzle and near its eyes. Like other tyrannosaurs, it would stay quite still, waiting for its victims.

Albertosaurus

WHICH WERE THE MOST RUTHLESS PREDATORS?

Despite their small size, some predators of the Mesozoic Era were the most fierce and ruthless killers. The Velociraptor, ('fast predator') for example was less than 2 metres long and only as tall as a small child. But with its slender build it could run very fast in pursuit of mammals and plant-eating dinosaurs. Once it reached its prey, the Velociraptor would tear its victims to pieces with its deadly claws and sharp teeth.

The Deinonychus ('terrible claw') was about 3 metres long, and the same height as a man. It had excellent eyesight and chased its victims on its agile and muscular hind legs with its tail outstretched and rigid. It could reach speeds of 40km per hour. On the second finger of each foot it had a deadly, flexible claw, about 12cm long, which it would use to rip open its prey.

● HOW WHEN WHAT WHY ●

An unusual position?

The powerful muscles in the feet of the *Deinonychus* enabled it to keep the toe with the deadly claw raised up, whilst keeping the other toes on the ground. This prevented the claw becoming damaged by the rough ground.

HOW THEY KILLED

Whilst attacking their prey, both the *Velociraptor* and the *Deinonychus* could hold the victim with just one limb, whilst ripping it open with the other.

Q·U·I·Z

Find the hidden predator in each group.

1) ❏ Gallimimus ❏ Coelophysis ❏ Mussaurus
2) ❏ Plateosaurus ❏ Triceratops ❏ Eoraptor
3) ❏ Megalosaurus ❏ Iguanodon ❏ Stegoceras
4) ❏ Apatosaurus ❏ Camptosaurus ❏ Troodon

Answers
1) Coelophysis 2) Eoraptor 3) Megalosaurus
4) Troodon

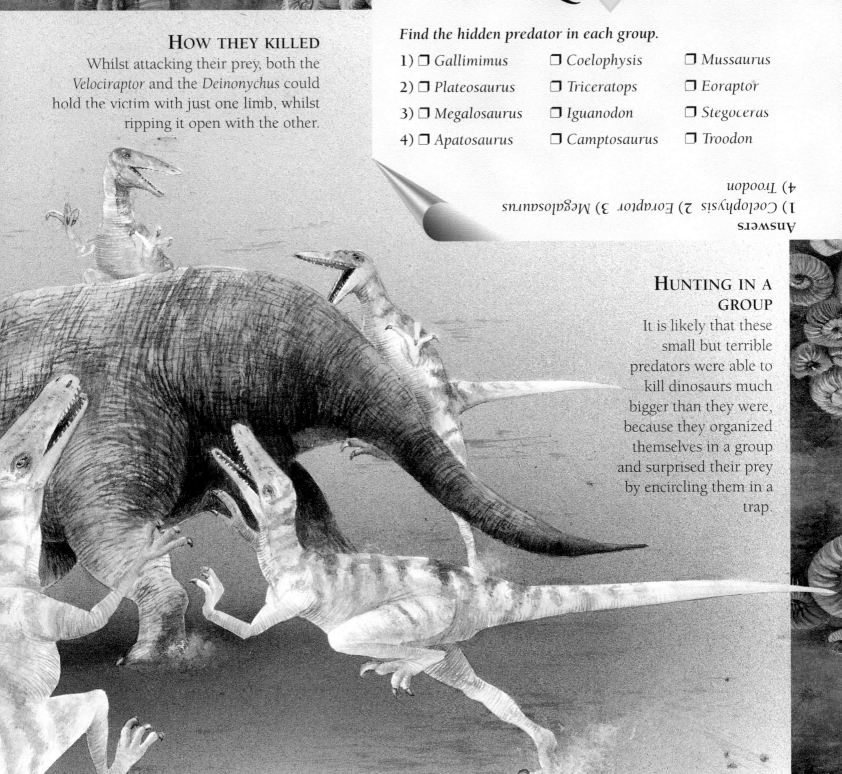

HUNTING IN A GROUP

It is likely that these small but terrible predators were able to kill dinosaurs much bigger than they were, because they organized themselves in a group and surprised their prey by encircling them in a trap.

Allosaurus

WAS THE ALLOSAURUS A PREDATOR?

Not only was the *Allosaurus* a fierce predator, it also had fearsome dimensions - weighing more than 1000kg, with a height of 4.5 metres and 12 metres long.

Its enormous mouth had 70 very sharp teeth and the fourth 'finger' on each limb ended with a strong, sharp claw. The *Allosaurus* ran at quite a speed, with lengthy strides which enabled it to reach its prey in just a few bounds.

HOW MANY DINOSAURS HAD CRESTS?

Many hadrosaurs (duck-billed dinosaurs) which lived in the Cretaceous Period had spectacular, huge crests of various sizes on their heads. There have been many different theories about the purpose of these crests. Some scientists believe that they helped hadrosaurs to hear sounds which were signs of danger, and were also a way of one hadrosaur recognizing another. Some believe the crest was used in courtship. According to others, the crests could also have helped hadrosaurs to forge their way through tangled vegetation.

HOW DID THE HADROSAURS LIVE?

There were many hadrosaurs of different appearances living throughout the whole of the planet. Usually four-legged, when danger threatened they ran on their back legs, with the tail outstretched to keep their balance. They had highly developed senses, which enabled them to be aware of danger in time to escape. Some threw themselves into water from the moment they learned how to swim. Hadrosaurs probably lived and nested in groups.

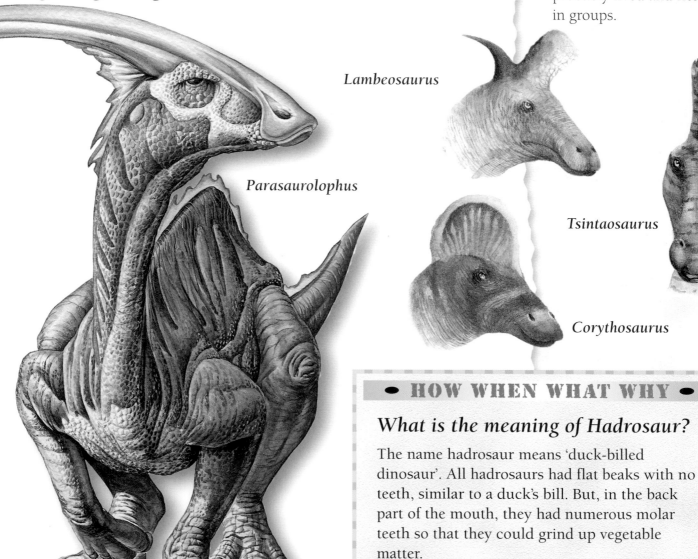

Lambeosaurus

Parasaurolophus

Tsintaosaurus

Corythosaurus

• HOW WHEN WHAT WHY •

What is the meaning of Hadrosaur?

The name hadrosaur means 'duck-billed dinosaur'. All hadrosaurs had flat beaks with no teeth, similar to a duck's bill. But, in the back part of the mouth, they had numerous molar teeth so that they could grind up vegetable matter.

WAS THE STEGOCERAS AGGRESSIVE?

The Stegoceras was generally a peaceful plant-eating dinosaur belonging to the pachycephalosaur ('narrow-head reptile') group. Like others in this group, the Stegoceras had a narrow, bony cap which covered the top part of its skull. Males in the same herd would fight fiercely, head to head, to win a mate, or to become leader of the herd. In battle with predators, the bony skull cap could be used as a weapon both in attack and defence.

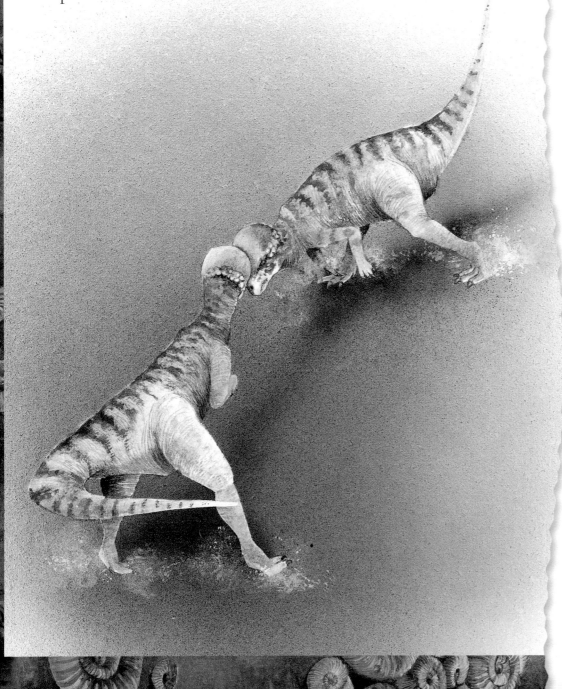

Stegoceras
- Height: 1.5 metres
- Length: 2.5 metres
  - Thickness of skull cap: 6 cm
    - Length of skull: 25cm

THE FAMILY OF PACHYCEPHALOSAURS

There were many types and many sizes of pachycephalosaurs. But all were characterized by the distinctive skull cap. The *Pachycephalosaurus* with a length of 5 metres was one of the largest in the group. Its skull cap was 25cm thick and edged with a bony ridge.

The *Prenocephalus* was 2.5 metres long. Its skull cap was encircled by bony spikes, similar to studs.

In the place of a cap the *Homalocephalus* (3 metres long) had two straight bony ridges at the top of its skull.

WHY DID DINOSAURS DIE OUT?

Despite the warm climate, plenty of food for both the plant-eaters and meat-eaters and the perfect way in which they had adapted to their surroundings, dinosaurs became extinct in one mass, and over a short period of time, 65 million years ago. Pterosaurs and ichthyosaurs, plesiosaurs and ammonites also disappeared at the same time.

There are many theories as to why they all became extinct. One of the most recent is that a gigantic meteor fell to Earth, causing explosions, sea-quakes, strong winds and a sharp rise in the climate temperature. The atmosphere would have been filled with dust which blotted out the light and the heat of the Sun for months, perhaps years, causing the death of many forms of animal and plant life.

● HOW WHEN WHAT WHY ●

How many other theories are there?

It has been suggested that it was the impact of a comet and not a meteor which caused vast clouds of dust. This theory is weak, because comets are made up of ice and dust - so a comet would not have had the energy to cause such a phenomenon.

Some believe that the extinction was due to one extraordinary burst of volcanic activity, which would have strongly affected the climate.

Another theory is that there may have been the widespread growth of poisonous plants or the spread of a deadly disease.

Animals

HOW MANY ANIMALS ARE THERE?

There are about two million living species in the animal kingdom and all have some features in common. All animals are multi-celled organisms, they can move the whole or part of the body, swallow food, get rid of their own waste material and they can reproduce. The variety of animals is amazing - sponges, bees, snakes, elephants, butterflies, parrots... some flying, some walking, others swimming, crawling, jumping... Vertebrates, including fish, reptiles, amphibians, mammals and birds, represent only 1.1% of all species of animals, whilst arthropods, a class which includes insects, crustaceans and arachnids, has the most species - over one million!

VERTEBRATES
This classification divides animals into two large groups - those with a spine or backbone (vertebrates) and those without a spine (invertebrates).

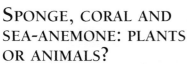

• HOW WHY WHAT WHEN •

How are animals classified?
Here is an example: the classification of a puma.
Kingdom: animal
Phylum (major group): chordata
Class: mammal
Order: carnivore
Family: cat
Genus: *felis*
Species: *puma concolor*

SPONGE, CORAL AND SEA-ANEMONE: PLANTS OR ANIMALS?
All animals must get food. But some sea creatures spend their lives anchored to rocks.

The sea-anemone, which looks like a flower, has small, stinging tentacles with which it poisons its prey before taking it into the body. And although it may seem quite still, the sea-anemone moves very, very slowly along a rock, thanks to the small suckers on the base of its body.

96

- There are over 9000 known species of birds.
- Reptiles comprise one of the largest groups of animals, with over 6000 species. Snakes, tortoises and crocodiles belong to this group.
- There are about 4200 species of amphibians. Frogs, toads, newts and salamanders are all amphibians.
- There are more than 23000 species of fish in many shapes, colours and sizes.
- There are about 4600 species in the group of mammals, from the huge elephant to the tiny dormouse.

PHYLUM

Phylum is the term for a major group of animals. There are 35 phyla. The main ones are - Chordata (which includes verterbrates), Porifera (sponges), Molluscs (oysters, octopus), Coelenterata (jellyfish), Arthropods (insects, spiders, scorpions), Echinodermata (starfish, sea-urchin).

Coral is a tiny little sea creature with a soft body and tentacles. All around itself it makes a calcium shelter, which it never leaves. To capture its prey, it stretches out its stinging tentacles from inside its 'hideout'.

Sponges live anchored to rocks or clasped to the shells of hermit crabs. They absorb nutriments by filtering water through their pores.

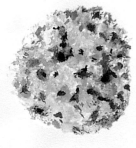

97

WHICH ARE THE LARGEST ANIMALS IN THE WORLD?

The Blue Whale, with a length of 30m and a weight of 130 tonnes (equal to the weight of 20 elephants!) is the largest living animal.

The largest land mammal is the African Elephant, with a height of 4m and a weight of 7 tonnes.

The largest carnivore (meat-eater) is the Brown Bear, which can grow to a height of 3m, with a weight of 750kg.

The longest snake is the Python (up to 10m). The heaviest snake is the Anaconda, which can weigh more than 100kg.

Among the largest fish is the Whale Shark, 15m long and weighing 18 tonnes.

The largest living invertebrate is the Giant Squid, with a length of up to 18-20m and a weight of 2 tonnes.

WHAT IS THE LARGEST FROG ON EARTH?

The common frog, widespread throughout Europe, grows to a maximum length of 9cm. The Goliath Frog which lives in African rivers is huge - it can reach up to 40cm in length. In Central Asia lives another giant amphibian - the bullfrog, with a length of 20cm. The bullfrog is a greedy hunter, feeding on smaller frogs, snakes, earthworms and insects.

• HOW WHY WHAT WHEN •

Which is the tallest animal?

Because of its long neck, the giraffe towers over all other animals on Earth. A male giraffe can grow to 5.8m. The tallest bird is the ostrich, which can grow to a height of 2.5m.

WHICH ANIMAL IS THE FASTEST?

The fastest animal of all is the cheetah which can reach an incredible speed of 96km per hour over short distances. This high speed is beaten only in the air. The Peregrine Falcon, the fastest bird in the world, pursues its prey at a breathtaking speed of 200km per hour, whilst the swift can fly at 60km per hour, even over longer distances. In water, the fastest animal is the Sail Fish which can reach speeds of 100km per hour.

WHAT IS THE SLOWEST ANIMAL?

The slowness of the snail and the slug is legendary. But the slow speed of the sloth, a large herbivore (plant-eater) which lives in the tropical forests of Central America is almost unbelievable. This mammal spends its day drowsing, hanging from the branches of trees by its paws. When it descends the tree, it moves so slowly that its speed is never faster than about 2.5 cm per minute.

• HOW WHY WHAT WHEN •

What speeds can a dog reach?

Many breeds of dog which were once bred for hunting are now more common as pets than hunting dogs. A Greyhound can run at speeds of up to 64km per hour, whilst the Weimaraner, once used for hunting large prey such as wolves and wild boar, can reach speeds of up to 56km per hour in a chase.

WHICH IS THE MOST DANGEROUS ANIMAL?

The most dangerous animals are the poisonous ones. Some of them can produce a venom (poison) powerful enough to kill a man - like the small Blue-Ringed Octopus, seemingly harmless, but which, after biting its victim, squirts poison on the wound, causing failure of the nervous system and leading to death. The scorpion has a sting in its tail which it uses to paralyse its prey and kill it. A scorpion attacks human beings only in self-defence. The venom from many of the larger scorpions can kill a person in just a few hours. A bite from the female Black Widow spider, the most deadly of all spiders and recognizable by the red spots on a black abdomen, causes terrible pain, difficulty in breathing and sometimes even death. The most dangerous snake on land is the Indian Cobra. Its bite can kill within 20 minutes.

● HOW WHY WHAT WHEN ●

What colour is the Coral Snake?

Particularly dangerous because of its venom is the Small Coral Snake. Its vivid colours may warn some animals about how dangerous it is. Many of its victims are large, attracted by its bright colours and its small size. That is why in parts of America children are taught a nursery rhyme so that they can distinguish a coral snake from others which are similar but harmless. 'If yellow touches red, run fast, or you're dead. If red touches black, then you're on the right track.'

On a square piece of paper draw a curled-up coral snake. Colour it in, as shown in the picture. Cut out around the spirals, then make a little hole in the centre of the snake's head. Thread a piece of string through the hole and fasten with a knot on the underside. Tie the other end of the thread to a little stick. Hold it up above a source of heat (an electric hot-plate or a radiator) and you will see the snake moving and twirling around.

WHERE DO THEY LIVE?
The Blue-Ringed Octopus lives around the Australian Great Barrier Reef. Scorpions are widespread throughout hot, dry regions. The Black Widow spider is found in the hot areas of America and Southern Europe.

WHICH SEA CREATURE IS THE MOST DANGEROUS TO HUMAN BEINGS?
The White Shark is a very fierce predator, which will sometimes attack human beings. With its tremendously strong jaws and two rows of jagged teeth arranged like a triangle in its mouth, it devours its prey in just a few mouthfuls, swallowing it almost whole.

The Stone Fish, which gets its name because of its ability to blend in perfectly with the rocky beds of tropical seas, lives in waters which are not too deep. If a swimmer hits the Stone Fish by accident, the fish pricks up its dorsal fin which can inject the person with a dose of deadly poison.

How do birds fly?

Birds can beat their wings to fly because of their powerful pectoral (chest) muscles. By pushing the air towards the ground, a bird rises up, moving forward by pushing the air behind it. The wings lift it up, with the feathers open to cut through the air, and brings the bird down with the feathers closed to push it towards the ground. Wings are shaped differently, according to different forms of flying. With their large and wide wings, eagles and vultures can reach great heights and glide with currents of air. The narrow pointed wings of the swift are perfect for rapid, continuous flight, whilst pheasants have wide, rounded wings, ideal for a rapid but short flight. Some birds, such as the dove, have to move their wings almost continuously to support the weight of the body. Other, smaller birds alternate actual flying with gliding. Instead of the usual vibrating movement of the wings, a Hummingbird keeps its wings rigid, but flapping them very, very rapidly. This enables it to remain quite still in the air and even to fly backwards.

NOT ONLY FOR FLIGHT
As well as flying, birds can move in other ways to get food or to flee from danger. Some walk or jump, others run and some swim.

• HOW WHY WHAT WHEN •

Can all birds fly?

Although all birds have wings, not all can fly. The ostrich is a very fine runner, fleeing from enemies at speeds of up to 65km per hour. A penguin uses its wings as flippers, making it a great swimmer. The flightless kiwi has only tiny, poorly developed wings hidden among its feathers. A chicken can just about manage to rise up from the ground.

CHARACTERISTICS

All birds are covered in feathers, they have two wings and a beak, with no teeth. The legs of larger birds are covered with scales.

Look at the picture below and copy the different feathers on a thin sheet of paper. Colour them, cut out and then you can try and make a bird's wing, arranging the feathers as shown, with the small down feathers and then the plumage.

covert feathers

quill feathers

HOW IS A FEATHER FORMED?

A feather is made of keratin, a flexible substance which is also present in our fingernails, in skins and in animal horns. Hundreds of barbs are joined to the central shaft of the feather and these form a compact surface. The barbs are kept together by tiny little hooks, called barbules.

The long quill feathers are at the edge of the wing. The covert feathers, on top, give the wing its shape and makes it waterproof. The down feathers, short and soft, are next to the bird's flesh and keep the body warm.

Is it only birds that fly?

The Flying Squirrel has a thin membrane of skin attached to each side of its body, between the front and rear legs and covered with fur. When this rodent jumps from one tree to another, it opens out its limbs, rather like a parachute, and is able to glide up more than 400m, using its tail both as a rudder and as a brake.

A Flying Fish jumps out of the water by a strong flip of its tail and it can remain in the air for up to 10m, using its wide pectoral fins which it can open out like wings. The tree frog makes long jumps between trees and glides for a few metres, by means of a membrane of skin which joins up its 'fingers'.

- The largest bat is the Flying Fox, which gets its name because of the shape of its nose. Some found on the island of Java have a wing span of 1.7m with a length of up to 42cm.

- The smallest bat lives in Thailand. It weighs just 2 grammes and is no longer than 3.3cm.

HOW DOES THE BAT FLY?

The bat is the only mammal which can really fly, like a bird. The structure of the sectors of its wings allows the bat to fly, although at a slow speed, but with remarkable powers of movement. The wings are formed by one thin layer of skin without fur and which joins the top claws to either side of the body.

The bat is a nocturnal animal. During the day it stays with its wings folded, hanging upside down from the branches of trees or inside caves or attics.

IN WHICH PARTS OF THE WORLD DO MAMMAL LIVE?

Mammals can adapt to every type of climate, from the polar circles to the Equator, and so they are widespread throughout the world. Thick skins, hibernation, migration and the ability to collect food are only a few of the ways in which mammals cope with the different conditions of the places where they live.

IN THE DESERT...

The camel is very well adapted to live in the desert, due to the considerable quantity of fat in its hump and on which it can live when there is little food and water. Its large feet stop the camel from slipping on the sand.

...AND ON THE SNOW

Among the freezing landscape of the arctic plain (the tundra) lives the Musk Ox. To find food, it digs in the snow and ice with its hoofs, searching for moss, lichen and roots.

• HOW WHY WHAT WHEN •

What are mammals like?

Mammals are warm-blooded animals, which means they have a constant body temperature. All mammals are covered with hair of different thicknesses and give birth to living young which feed on milk produced by the mammary glands of the female. A mammal has a well-developed brain and takes care of its young for a long time. The only mammals which lay eggs are the Platypus and the Spiny-Coated Echidna, but both suckle their young.

DO ALL ANIMALS CARE FOR THEIR YOUNG?

Different animals behave in different ways when it comes to rearing their young. Some rear their young in pairs, others alone, others do not take care of their young at all. Whatever happens, the species will not die out. Frogs and tortoises, for example, leave their eggs after laying them. But the number of eggs is so great that at least some are bound to survive. Vipers and rattle-snakes give birth to young which are already independent, so they need take no care of them. The female cobra on the other hand is the only snake which takes care of her young, even though they are fully independent as soon as they are born. Other animals, such as mammals and birds care for their young for a long time.

SMALL PREDATORS

The Nile Crocodile lays her eggs in a hole. When they are ready to hatch, the babies make a special sound, as a sign to the mother that the time has arrived for them to come out of the eggs. They are predators as soon as they are born!

• HOW WHY WHAT WHEN •

How long does the Emperor Penguin sit on its eggs?

The male Emperor Penguin sits on its egg for about two months. During this time it keeps the egg under its feet, covering it with a fold of his skin, not only to protect it from the cold, but also so that it will not fall on the ice. This process means that the male Emperor Penguin has to go without food the whole time, until the baby penguin hatches!

1) Which of these animals do you think continue to live in a community after giving birth?
❏ bees ❏ frogs ❏ tigers

2) Which of these animals gives birth to four identical babies and all of them the same sex?
❏ platypus ❏ armadillo ❏ cobra

3) How many months does the tigress spend bringing up her cubs?
❏ 12 ❏ 6 ❏ 15

4) How many years does a baby orang-utan remain with its mother?
❏ 1 ❏ 3 ❏ 5

5) Which bird lays its eggs in a common nest with other females?
❏ owl ❏ swift ❏ ostrich

Answers
1) bees 2) armadillo 3) 6 4) 5 5) ostrich

DOES ONLY THE FEMALE LOOK AFTER THE YOUNG?

In only a few cases, it is the male animal which looks after the young, after taking inside him eggs laid by the female. For example, the female sea-horse lays her eggs in the stomach pouch of the male. After about 15 days the male sea-horse prepares to give birth. Anchored to a frond of seaweed by its tail, it gives birth to as many as 200 babies and the process can last more than a day. In Chile, the male Darwin's Frog takes care of the tadpoles as soon as they begin moving, taking them into his vocal sac, and keeping them there until they are ejected from his mouth as small, perfectly-formed frogs.

WHY DOES THE KANGAROO HAVE A POUCH?

The female kangaroo has a pouch on her stomach, because, unlike other mammals, she cannot carry her babies inside her until they are fully developed. So, after the birth, the tiny kangaroo, as yet without fur, blind and only 3cm long, climbs up the mother's body until it reaches her pouch. Here, suckled by the mother kangaroo's mammary glands, it grows until, seven months later, it can leave the mother.

● HOW WHY WHAT WHEN ●

Where do marsupials live?

Most marsupials (animals with pouches) live in Australia, because they remained isolated here following the sub-division of the Pangea. Some species are spread throughout Guinea, and the Opossum lives mainly in North America.

WHICH ANIMALS HAVE POUCHES?

There are many marsupials - more than 270 species!
The young of the Koala Bear, when they leave the pouch, scramble up the back of the mother, living attached to her among the branches of trees.
The Tasmanian Devil is a meat-eating marsupial which hunts at night. It is also a very fine swimmer.
The Opossum is not really a true marsupial, but has a sort of double fold of skin around the mammary glands. When the young are big enough, they are brought up in a nest.

The Wombat digs a long tunnel to build an underground lair. Its pouch is turned inwards, so that it does not get filled with loose soil.

IN WHAT WAYS DO ANIMALS DISGUISE THEMSELVES?

Some animals can disguise themselves to blend in with the surroundings where they live, taking on shapes and colours to prevent them being seen by predators. The leaf insect and some stick insects, like the cicada, take on the shape and the colour of leaves, a branch or a bush, so that they are not seen by insect-eating animals. The ermine and the hare, to escape their predators, change the colour of their coat during the winter, becoming as white as the snowy landscape. The down feathers of jays, woodcocks and pheasants are the same colours as the undergrowth. Another type of disguise is that of the Viceroy Butterfly. To avoid being eaten, it takes on the colours of the Monarch Butterfly, which has a sour taste and so it is left alone by the birds.

● HOW WHY WHAT WHEN ●

How does the chameleon change colour?

The skin of the chameleon is rich in pigment (colour) cells and so it can change colour because of the light, the temperature of its surroundings or the mood of the animal. When the colour of the chameleon's skin adapts to its surroundings, it can become invisible, not only to its predators, but also to its prey. If the animal is disturbed or if it wants to escape an intruder it becomes dark, to show that it is in.... a black mood!

WHY IS A ZEBRA'S COAT STRIPED?

All zebras do not have the same sort of stripes. Some species have distinctive patterns of stripes which distinguish them from other zebras. The zebra's stripes are a means of disguise, because they make it more difficult for the predator to pick out one animal in a group. And at dusk, the zebras become almost invisible at a certain distance, because their stripes merge with the surrounding landscape.

109

WHY ARE SOME ANIMALS MULTI-COLOURED?

Many male birds display the bright colours of their plumage to attract the female. Almost always, females have much quieter colours - useful as a disguise when they are sitting on their nests and caring for their young. For some poisonous animals with dangerous ways of defending themselves, like stings or spines, bright colours make them more noticeable and put enemies on their guard, warning them to stay away. Some predators use experience to learn which prey to avoid. The colours which normally signal danger are red and yellow, with black.

THE SCORPION FISH
The Scorpion Fish is widespread throughout the Red Sea and the Pacific Ocean, signalling its poisonous stings with bright colours.

• HOW WHY WHAT WHEN •

Why is the flamingo pink?

The flamingo feeds on shrimps, which contain a remarkable amount of carotene - a pigment which produces a colour between orange and red. Due to the digestion of the shrimps and their carotene, the plumage of the flamingo keeps its splendid colour. That is why in the zoos and parks where flamingos are kept, a portion of shrimps is regularly added to their food.

1) Which insects use a luminous sign to communicate between male and female?

2) Which plant-eating mammal has on its back a spot the same colour as one on its nose?

3) Which mammals uses the sharp contrast between white and black to keep enemies away?

Answers
1) fireflies 2) gazelle 3) skunk

WHAT IS A FALSE EYE?

In order to mislead predators and prey, some animals have one or two dark spots on their bodies which look rather like an eye. Some have this 'false eye' on their tail. Then if they are attacked from behind, they have time to escape.

false eye

Many butterflies have large circular spots on their wings. Seen from a distance, a spot can be mistaken for an eye and this confuses the butterfly's enemies.

YELLOW AND BLACK

The Yellow and Black Salamander has a poisonous skin. Its surface colour puts its predators on guard. Bees use the same colours to warn 'enemies' that their sting can be dangerous.

ARROW-POISON TOAD

This toad is widespread throughout Central and South America. The toad only has to show enemies its brightly coloured red and yellow stomach to scare them away!

111

How does the polar bear hunt?

The vast expanse of ice at the North Pole means that the Polar Bear often has to walk 10km in search of its favourite food, the seal. The Polar Bear needs to eat at least one every six days. To capture its prey, the Polar Bear will sit motionless for hours watching the hole in the ice where the seal will eventually come up for air. And the moment the seal appears, with a lightning movement the Polar Bear seizes it in its powerful claws and bites into it, before dragging it across the ice. But if the seal is on pack ice (a mass of floating ice), the Polar Bear will swim silently towards it, the last few metres underwater. Then, with a sudden bound, it will emerge from the water and hurl itself at its prey.

A WANDERING CARNIVORE
The Arctic Wolf is a wanderer which can cover distances of hundreds of kilometres across land. During the winter, it wanders across the ice, feeding on the carcasses and remains left by Polar Bears. The thick fur which insulates the wolf against the cold is white in winter but brown in summer.

EXCELLENT SENSE OF SMELL
The fur of the seal cub may blend in very well with the white snow. But it cannot beat the excellent sense of smell of the Polar Bear.

A FINE SWIMMER
The Polar Bear is a tireless swimmer. Protected by its fat and its thick fur, it can swim up to 80km without stopping.

WHICH ARE THE BIGGEST CATS?

Lions and tigers are the largest cats in existence. With their acute senses, strong bodies, sharp teeth and claws, they are formidable hunters. With lions, it is nearly always the lioness that hunts, often in a group with other lionesses. Tigers are solitary animals, and hunt by night. To reach their prey, these big cats can also swim across rivers. They kill their prey by biting the neck, before dragging it to the place where they want to eat it.

DIMENSIONS
A lion can reach a length of 3m and weigh up to 250kg. A tiger can grow to around 3.6 metres, with a weight of up to 350kg.

OTHER BIG CATS
A cheetah is an exceptional runner, with an agile and streamlined body and long legs.

The jaguar is widespread in South America. It has a spotted coat and is an excellent swimmer.

The Panther Leopard can either be completely black, or have a yellow coat with black spots.

The puma, also called the cougar and the mountain lion, is a solitary hunter living in parts of North and South America. Its coat can be reddish or greyish yellow.

How do fish breathe underwater?

Like all animals, fish need to breathe oxygen in order to live. That is why they have gills - two openings, one either side of the head, and through which a fish can absorb the oxygen in the water. When its gills are closed, the fish takes in water through its mouth. As the water flows over the gills, the oxygen filters through the thin gill membranes and is absorbed by the blood vessels. Then the water flows out through the open gills, taking the carbon dioxide with it. Fish open and close their gills to much the same rhythm as animals on land breathe in and out.

PROTECTION FOR THE GILLS
The bony layer which covers each gill is called the 'operculum'. It protects the delicate filaments of the gills.

● HOW WHY WHAT WHEN ●

How do mammals breathe underwater?

Whales and dolphins have a respiratory system similar to other animals. They have lungs and so can breathe in oxygen in the air. That is why they have to come out of the water at regular intervals and breathe in though the nostrils which are at the side of the head. Dolphins often breathe in oxygen during their characteristic leaps and jumps.

HOW MANY WAYS CAN FISH SWIM?
Fish move about in horizontal ripples (from side to side), using both the body and the fins. The movement of the tail helps the fish to go forward. The eel contracts and then releases its muscles, going along in a series of winding, curving movements. By changing the direction of the contractions, it can also move backwards.

Q·U·I·Z

1) Which of these fish do you think lives in rivers?

❑ trout   ❑ sole   ❑ mullet

2) Which fish lives in lakes?

❑ cod   ❑ bream   ❑ perch

3) Which fish can give an electric shock?

❑ stingray   ❑ moray eel   ❑ eel

4) Which fish swims upright?

❑ clown fish   ❑ pilot fish   ❑ sea-horse

Answers
1) trout 2) perch 3) stingray
4) sea-horse

Marine mammals swim rapidly using the vertical movement of their tails, which give them a powerful push forward. The ray swims by 'waving' its wide pectoral fins.

115

IS THE OCTOPUS INTELLIGENT?

The octopus is a highly developed mollusc which can change its behaviour as it learns from experience. In a marine aquarium an octopus will show that it recognizes the person who brings it food. Many tests have proved the ability of the octopus to recognize shapes and to follow a pre-set course. It is a solitary animal which lives in coral reefs and among rocks near to the coast. Acute eyesight and a wonderful ability to disguise itself are two means of defence for the octopus. The third and most famous is to squirt inky fluid, to confuse an enemy's sense of direction.

- An octopus has 8 tentacles.
- On average an octopus weighs about 3kg. Some larger examples can weigh up to 10kg.
- It can open its tentacles up to 2 or 3 metres wide.
- An octopus can grow to a length of between 1 and 1.3 metres.
- It lays between 100,000 and 500,000 eggs.
- At birth it measures only 3mm.

HOW DOES AN OCTOPUS SWIM?

Like the squid and the cuttlefish, an octopus, when it wants to swim, fills an internal muscular cavity with water. It empties this cavity by forcing the water out through a small opening called a spout. With each jet of water, the octopus goes forward or backward, according to the direction of the spout. The more stronger and rapid the jets of water, the faster the animal moves.

HOW DOES A BUTTERFLY DEVELOP?

The life cycle of a butterfly begins with an egg and then goes through various stages. From the egg hatches the larva, or caterpillar, which we see feeding on leaves as it grows. When the caterpillar is fully-grown, it turns into a chrysalis by spinning a cocoon around itself with its own thread. Inside the chrysalis, usually fastened to a branch or a leaf, the butterfly develops wings, antennae and little legs. When the butterfly is fully developed, it breaks out of the chrysalis and spreads its wings to dry itself and to start the blood flowing. After a night of rest, it can then fly.

WHAT IS A MOTH?

Like the butterfly, the moth belongs to the order *lepidoptera* (insects). They are very similar, but there are some differences. Almost all butterflies are active by day, they have threadlike antennae and no scales. A butterfly rests keeping its wings in an upright position on top of its body. Its wings are usually brightly-coloured. The moth 'comes to life' at night. Its antennae are often feather-like and when it is at rest, it keeps its wings flat against its back. Its wings are generally dark coloured, such as grey and brown.

FEEDING

A butterfly and a moth feed by sucking the nectar from flowers through a proboscis - an opening in its mouth.

HOW MANY CLASSES OF BEES ARE THERE IN A HIVE?

The queen bee is about 2cm long, with a long body and a fat abdomen. She has a sting which she can use many times throughout her life, and is the only bee which can lay eggs. Worker bees are smaller and can use their stings only once, because the force needed for it to push the sting out of its body and into the victim causes a fatal gash. The worker bee sucks nectar from flowers by means of a tiny proboscis and collects the nectar inside a sac in its abdomen. Its hind legs have little hairs which collect pollen from the flowers.

The male bee, the drone, is squat and thickset. It does not have a sting, and its only function is to fertilize the queen. As soon as this has been done, the drone dies. All bees have antennae, and two pairs of wings.

INSECTS

All insects have a body divided into three sections - the head, thorax and abdomen - and six legs. Many species among the 800,000 listed have wings. Insects are the most numerous group of living things.

• HOW WHY WHAT WHEN •

How do bees comminicate?

A bee can communicate to others where it has found a source of food by going through two types of dance, which it does inside the hive. If the food is less than 100 metres away, the dance is circular. If the food is more than 100 metres away, then the dance is in the form of a figure of 8. By using particular dance patterns, a bee can communicate not only the distance of the food but also the direction to follow.

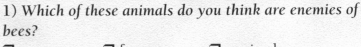

LIFE IN THE HIVE

Each hive is made up of hexagonal-shaped cells, each one a tiny nest. There is a queen, hundreds of drones and thousands of workers. The queen can live up to 5 years, the workers 2 months and the drones only 4 weeks.

1) Which of these animals do you think are enemies of bees?
❒ wasps ❒ frogs ❒ squirrels

2) Which of these insects live in a community?
❒ flies ❒ butterflies ❒ ants

3) Which of these animals is not an insect?
❒ cockroach ❒ bug ❒ scorpion

4) Which of these insects also have a king or queen?
❒ ants ❒ termites ❒ wasps

5) Which insect does most harm to plants?
❒ aphid ❒ cicada ❒ the praying mantis

Answers
1) wasps 2) ants 3) scorpion 4) termites 5) aphid

WHAT DO BEES PRODUCE?

Bees build their hives with the wax produced by their own glands. Honey is the product of their work on the nectar, which they mix with their own digestive juices The honey is then stored in the cells of the hive. The taste of the honey varies according to the flowers from which the nectar has been taken. Royal Jelly, on which only the queen bee and new-born larvae feed, is also produced in the special glands of the worker bees. People keep bees to use their products for food and in the home.

IS THE SPIDER AN INSECT?

A spider is not an insect, but an arachnid. It has eight legs and its body is in two main parts, the head and the abdomen. Scorpions belong to the same class as spiders. There are more than 70,000 types of arachnid, almost all of them living on land. There are about 30,000 species of spiders, and all are predators. After a spider captures its prey, it bites into it. This bite releases a powerful poison from special glands inside the spider. The spider's poison paralyzes its prey. The spider then sucks out the juices and soft parts of the prey.

THE BLACK WIDOW
Only the female of this spider bites, the male is harmless. Her poison is fatal, more powerful than even the rattle-snake.

• HOW WHY WHAT WHEN •

How does a spider reproduce?

Usually, spiders lay their eggs on plants, protected by a spider's web. The eggs are watched over by the female, and she sometimes carries them with her in a cocoon of silk. When the baby spiders hatch, they stay for some time with the mother, then, hanging on to the last thread of silk, they let go, blown by the wind, in search of a place where they can settle.

• The Bird-Eating Tarantula is the largest spider. One found was reported to have had a leg span of 28cm, more or less the depth of this page.

• The smallest spider is only as big as a punctuation mark, less than half a millimetre.

• There are some spiders which only lay 1-3 eggs. Others, like the Mygalomorph, lay over 3000.

• Some tropical spiders spin yellow and white silk, up to 3 metres long.

MYGALE

This is a species of bird-eating water spider which lives in South America. It moistens its prey with a liquid from its intestines. This liquid dissolves the tissue and reduces the prey to paste, ready for the spider to eat.

HOW DOES THE SPIDER SPIN ITS WEB?

By spinnerets, special organs in its abdomen, a spider can produce a strong thread which is fine enough to make a hardwearing web and which is also sticky, to capture its prey. The structure of the web takes about an hour's work.

1) The spider stretches the first thread between two points. Then it turns back...

2) The spider goes halfway along the thread, then produces a third thread, ready to stretch the web downwards.

3) The spider then adds spokes leading from the centre to make the basic design, moving itself along threads which it has already stretched around surrounding objects.

4) The spider then makes a spiral of sticky thread, leaving some threads free, so that it can move along these. It pulls the last thread, the 'signal thread', tight. This thread will then shake as soon as an insect gets stuck on the web.

HOW DO SNAKES KILL?

A constrictor snake kills by curling itself around its prey and crushing it until the victim suffocates. A Python can construct a young gazelle and swallow it whole. The digestion takes many days and ends with the snake spitting out all the undigested parts. The Boa Constrictor feeds on small animals and birds, which it eats starting from the head. The digestion of such animals is made possible by the snake's strong gastric juices which can even break down bone. Other snakes use their venom to paralyze or to kill their prey. The most dangerous, such as the viper and the cobra, have poisonous fangs in the front of their mouth and which they use not only to attack but also to defend themselves. Snakes with poisonous fangs in the back part of their mouth have a less powerful bite, because they only eat their prey if they have already seized it.

● HOW WHY WHAT WHEN ●

Do snakes have highly developed senses?

The hearing and the sight of the snake is not very good. It is led to its prey more by its sense of smell. A snake can detect the presence of prey also by extending its fangs, which relays smells and tastes in the surrounding air back to a special organ in the snake's mouth. Some snakes have special ways of becoming aware of the heat given off by other animals.

HOW DO SNAKES MOVE?

Snakes can curl themselves up in different ways, because of their powerful muscles and the wonderful flexibility of their backbone. A snake can move like an accordion - that is, by bringing up its tail close to its head, then stretching out the head from the rest of the body. Then, it brings up its tail close to its head and repeats the movement.

moving horizontally

moving in a straight line

122

FACTS·AND·FIGURES

REPTILES

Snakes, like crocodiles and tortoises belong to the class of reptiles. All reptiles are vertebrates and cold-blooded - this means with a body temperature which depends on the temperature of the surroundings.

- The Gabon Viper, with a length of up to 2 metres, is the one of the longest snakes. Its poisonous fangs can be up to 5cm long.

- The venom of the King Cobra can kill a man in 15 minutes.

- The fastest sea snake can swim at 3.6km an hour.

- The Black Mamba is recorded as the fastest snake in the world, reaching speeds of 11km per hour.

- The quantity of venom which a Tiger Snake can use could kill 125,000 mice.

THE ANACONDA

The Anaconda is a giant snake of the Amazon region of South America. It can kill its prey by means of an immensely strong and immovable hold.

THE RATTLE-SNAKE

The Rattle-Snake is a very good hunter. It advances silently towards its victims then hits with a lightning blow...

Snakes can also move across stones or other objects by pushing first towards the right and then to the left, rather like a series of letter S. They can also move in a line when they place first the head and the tail together, then pointing with either the head or tail to move the body sideways.

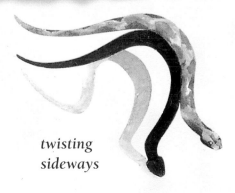

twisting sideways

This method of movement allows many snakes to live in desert regions where they have prolonged contact with burning sand. Other snakes move along by gripping the ground by means of the scales on their stomachs.

WHAT IS A TADPOLE?

Like most amphibians, the frog lays its eggs in the waters of ponds and marshes. Tadpoles hatch from these eggs - larvae which are similar to small fish and which breathe through gills. Tadpoles have a long tail and feed on algae (water-weed). After some weeks, the tadpole grows hind legs and then front legs. In time, the tail becomes shorter until it disappears altogether. The tadpole also develops lungs. And so the tadpole is transformed into a frog and begins its life on land, feeding on insects and worms, but always staying near water.

AMPHIBIANS
Amphibians are cold-blooded animals. They do not have fur or scales and breathe through their skin, which is smooth and damp, but with pores. Some amphibians are poisonous.

• HOW WHY WHAT WHEN •

How do frogs communicate?

In order to croak, both a male frog and a male toad gulps air into a vocal sac or sacs under the throat, making a very strong sound despite their under-developed lungs. The calls of the frog are different from one species to another and are used in courtship and to defend itself. Some poisonous frogs can be recognized not only by their colour but also their croak.

124

THE SALAMANDER

This amphibian has a tail and a body similar to the lizard. It lives on land, in trees and sometimes in the water.

- The Chinese Giant Salamander weighs up to 65kg and grows up to 1.8m long. Upright, it would be as tall as a man!

- The toad lays up to 6000 eggs, a long jelly-like chain up to 4m long.

- Only 20% of toads live for 5 years.

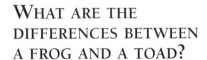

WHAT ARE THE DIFFERENCES BETWEEN A FROG AND A TOAD?

We can distinguish these animals by their skin and the way they move. The frog has a moist, smooth coat, because it is protected by a layer of mucus. It jumps with its hind legs which are longer and stronger than the front legs.

The toad has a dry, lumpy skin, sometimes covered with warts. Its hind legs, short and fat, means that it walks rather clumsily.

WHY IS THE GORILLA AT RISK OF EXTINCTION?

In the mountains of equatorial Africa, there are only a few thousand gorillas which have survived being hunted and the destruction of tropical forests which is their home. At one time they were captured by man to be reared in zoos or to be killed and eaten. Today there are special projects to find the few gorilla species which remain and to safeguard their habitat. Many other animals also risk extinction because of the damage and the changes to their natural surroundings, often the fault of humans.

HOW MANY ANIMALS ARE AT RISK OF EXTINCTION?

Many animals risk extinction, including – the Giant Panda, the Blue Whale, the Aye-Aye Ape of Madagascar, the Black Rhinoceros, the Queen Alexandra Birdwing butterfly, New Zealand's Kakapo Parrot, the Californian Condor and the Giant Turtle of the Galapagos Islands.

• HOW WHY WHAT WHEN •

How does a gorilla live?

Gorillas are peaceful but enormous (an adult can grow up to 2m in height). They live in groups of 5-20 individuals, with a chief in charge who decides where they settle and settles any dispute in the group. They are vegetarians and spend a good deal of time swinging from the branches of trees.

Plants

WHAT ARE PLANTS?

Plants are organisms which belong to the vegetable kingdom. Most plants are green, because they contain chlorophyll, a substance that can use energy from the Sun to make food. So far, there are over 400,000 species of plants with different structures, forms and sizes. Plants can be small and simple, like mosses or duckweed. Or they can be enormous and complex, like the Giant Sequoia tree. There are plants with flowers and without flowers, plants that lose their leaves each year, and plants which are evergreen. Many have a vascular system – a network of veins which transport water and nutriments to the inside of the plant.

THE ORIGIN

Plants originated from a group of green seaweed which about 450 million years ago adapted to life on land.

● HOW WHEN WHAT WHY ●

What is a plant cell like?

A plant cell has a strong outer wall of cellulose. At the centre is a cavity called the vacuole, which contains liquid. The nucleus and cytoplasm are outside the vacuole.
Other elements of the vegetable cell are chloroplasts (the organs which contain the green chlorophyll) the leucoplasts (which store nutriments) and chromoplasts which contain pigments of colours such as yellow, orange and red.

Cell

Q·U·I·Z

1) *What do you think are bryophytes?*
❏ plants without roots   ❏ plants without stems   ❏ grasses

2) *What is the scientific name for plants with flowers?*
❏ Gymnosperm   ❏ Pteridophyte   ❏ Angiosperm

3) *Which tree grows from an acorn?*
❏ beech   ❏ oak   ❏ willow

4) *What is a deciduous plant?*
❏ a plant with no flowers
❏ a plant which loses its leaves in autumn
❏ an evergreen plant

Answers
1) plants without roots 2) Angiosperm 3) oak
4) a plant which loses its leaves in autumn

WHERE DO PLANTS LIVE?

In the course of time, plants have adapted to all types of surroundings. Although ideal places are those with sufficient light, warmth and moisture, plants can survive in deserts and Polar regions.

In desert areas, plants have adapted to the hot, dry climate: their fleshy leaves hold a great quantity of water, and have a thick, waxy covering which stops evaporation.

NON-VASCULAR PLANTS

Some plants, such as moss, do not have an internal vascular system for the circulation of water. So they have to live in places where water is present, with the plant absorbing it directly from its surroundings.

Mosses and lichens live in the ice-free regions of the South Pole. Lichens are very hardy. According to the weather conditions, they can fall into a type of hiberation. Some plants live floating on water; the Water Lily has large, flat leaves, lovely white flowers and spread long roots down into the depths of slow-moving fresh water.

129

WHAT ARE TREES?

A tree is a plant which has a trunk protected by bark.
Most trees can grow to a height of several metres. Their
foliage is made up of leaves of many different shapes and
sizes – large and spreading, like the Oak, the Plane Tree
and the Chestnut, needle-shaped in Conifers, such as the
Pine, the Fir and the Cypress. Some species of trees,
which we call 'evergreens' do not lose their leaves.
Instead they change their foliage a little at a time in
rotation. Deciduous trees lose all their leaves once each
year, at the start of the coldest or driest season. Trees
usually develop roots at the base of the trunk.

THE CONIFER
The Conifer is the only
member of the larch family
which is evergreen. Its leaves
are covered with a dense
covering and they are in the
form of a needle to reduce
evaporation and exposure to
the cold to the minimum.

● HOW WHEN WHAT WHY ●

What is the bark?

The trunks of trees are protected by bark, a
dense layer of dead cells. The outermost part of
the bark is cork. The bark protects the tree
against insects, parasites and sharp changes in
temperature. There are also distinctive patterns
in the bark of each tree, and from one species to
another.

WHAT IS THE JOB OF THE ROOTS?
The roots absorb water from the soil, storing
nutriments to feed the leaves. Side roots
spreading out from the main root increase
absorption. Roots also keep the tree firmly in
the ground.

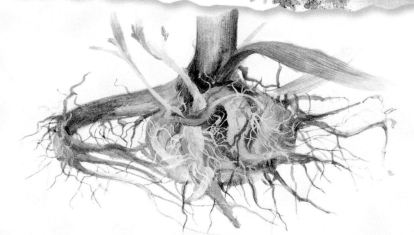

130

Each tree bark has a distinctive appearance, just like a person's fingerprint. To make a bark-rubbing, place a sheet of greaseproof or kitchen paper against part of a tree trunk where the bark can be seen clearly. Rub the paper with a wax pencil, keeping the paper flat, and you will get an 'imprint' of the bark. Do the same with other trees, then stick the rubbings on a piece of paper, with the name of the tree to which each bark-rubbing belongs.

BROAD-LEAVED TREES

Many broad-leaved trees are deciduous. Some tropical broad leaves trees keep their leaves all the year round.

Some roots conserve food as they grow and develop into root vegetables, such as the carrot. In some plants, the roots spread out into the water or the air. The roots of the Banyan Tree grow down from its branches, lengthening to the ground to form pillars.

131

WHY DO PLANTS NEED LIGHT?

Without light, plants could not make sugar. They absorb water and mineral salts from the soil and carbon dioxide from the air; all these elements are then combined inside and transformed into sugar. The sunlight, captured by the chlorophyll in the leaves, gives the plant the necessary energy for this chemical process, which is called photosynthesis.

Stoma

STOMATA
On the inner part of the leaf there are little pores called stomata. These enable the plant to absorb carbon dioxide and transform this into oxygen, which the plant then releases.

• HOW WHEN WHAT WHY •

What happens to plants at night-time?
During the day, a plant absorbs carbon dioxide and releases oxygen. But by night, in the absence of light, it absorbs oxygen and releases carbon dioxide and water vapour. The quantity of oxygen absorbed by night is less than the amount which the plant produces during the day.

Put two broad beans on a piece of damp cotton-wool and wait for them to start growing. When you see the beginnings of little plants, place these in two jars filled with soil. Put one jar near a window and the other in a cupboard, in the dark. Water both every three days, and measure their growth for two weeks. You will see that the plant in the dark starts growing quickly in search of the light, then the growth slows down and it becomes pale green. It will recover only if you put it in the light.

OXYGEN

The gas which plants release in the process of photosynthesis is oxygen, which human beings and animals need to keep breathing. It is thanks to plants that the percentage of oxygen in the atmosphere remains constant.

WHERE DOES THE SAP FLOW?

Sap is the 'lifeblood' of plants. It is water absorbed by the plant and contains sugar made by the plant itself, together with mineral salts. Inside the centre of the stem of vascular plants there are tube-like cells which enable the sap to flow. Those which carry the sap water and the mineral salts from the roots to the leaves (bottom to top) are the xylems. Those which take the sap to the tips of the roots (from top to bottom) are called the phloems. In a leaf, sap flows through the veins. The principal or main vein is at the centre, with thinner, secondary veins branching off to reach all parts of the leaf.

Phloem

Xylem

secondary vein

principal vein

133

HOW ARE LEAVES FORMED?

Plants have an astounding variety of leaves. In all parts of the world, leaves have developed different characteristics to adapt to different climates and to carry out their important task of making food for the whole plant. For example – the leaves of an evergreen plant are strong and covered with a waxy layer to resist downfalls of rain, wind, the hot Sun and insects. The leaves of some species which grow in dry regions have been 'transformed' into spines. In others the leaves are very small, so that they are exposed as little as possible to the intense heat. In the tropical forests, some leaves are gigantic, to attract as much sunlight as possible from the little which filters through the thick foliage of the trees.

• HOW WHEN WHAT WHY •

Why do some trees lose their leaves?

As they approach their most difficult season (the coldest or driest part of the year) deciduous trees lose their leaves, and so drastically reduce the amount of water that they need.
With the supply of sap interrupted, the leaves wither and fall from the branches. The branches survive on the food accumulated by the roots.
In spring, when the climate conditions become more favourable again, the plant produces new foliage.

CLASSIFICATION OF LEAVES

Leaves are distinguished mainly by their shape, which can be like an outspread hand, heart-shaped, oval or needle-shaped, pointed, wavy or fringed around the edges. Some leaves are simple, others compound – that is, formed of many little leaves.

Q·U·I·Z

Which plants do you think these leaves belong to?

1) ❏ basil
   ❏ mint
   ❏ sage

2) ❏ lime
   ❏ oak
   ❏ hazel

3) ❏ maple
   ❏ orange
   ❏ horse-chestnut

4) ❏ fig
   ❏ hazel
   ❏ geranium

Answers
1) basil 2) oak
3) maple 4) geranium

THE STALK

Leaves are usually joined to a woody twig by a stalk. Not all, though. In the Palm Tree, for example, leaves are attached directly to the trunk.

WHY DO LEAVES CHANGE COLOUR?

Most leaves are green because they contain chlorophyll. But many leaves also have pigments of other colours which form different patterns.

In the Holly bush, for example – if the chlorophyll is not distributed evenly, the foliage becomes variegated (patchy) in green and yellow.

In autumn, when the tree prepares itself for a rest from photosynthesis, the chlorophyll breaks down and other pigments appear in the leaves.

Some varieties of Beech and Hazel have red leaves.

WHY ARE SOME PLANTS MEAT-EATERS?

Most plants absorb the substances which they need from the ground. But in order to survive in dry or non-fertile areas, some have developed the capacity to eat insects or small animals such as frogs, from which they receive vitamins and mineral salts. Insects are attracted by the perfume and the colour of a plant and are then trapped by different methods – for instance, by being caught in the drops of the sticky 'glue' of Sundew, or imprisoned in the spiny lobes of a Venus Fly Trap.

How does a plant digest an animal?

Inside a 'meat-eating' plant there are special glands which produce the enzymes necessary to 'dissolve' the prey, so that the plant can absorb it. Enzymes are substances produced by living things and which cause the chemical reaction necessary for essential functions, such as digestion, reproduction and breathing.

WHICH PLANTS ARE MEAT EATERS?

The leaves of the Nepenthes Pitcher Plant are called ascidiums. These are like bags.

An insect, attracted by the nectar on the brim of the bag, goes to suck it up and is imprisoned inside. Bristles in the ascidium are turned downwards, and this stops the insect climbing back up.

The leaves of the Sundew are covered with green or red hairs which produce drops of sticky liquid, rather like drops of dew. When an insect lands on the leaf, it sticks to these hairs. The hairs then close together and imprison the insect.

At the first contact with its prey, the Venus Fly Trap immediately closes its spiny lobes, trapping the insect inside.

WHICH PLANTS ARE POISONOUS?

Flowers, leaves or fruit of some plants contain substances which are poisonous to animals and to human beings. These plants grow in all environments and are often used by people in floral decoration, as with the Oleander (Rose Bay) or Laburnum, or in the preparation of medicines – such as atropine from Deadly Nightshade or digitalis from the Foxglove. Other plants such as the stinging nettle contain toxic substances which cause a painful irritation on contact with the skin. Taken inwardly, these can even cause death by poisoning.

ARE POISONOUS PLANTS USEFUL?

The poisonous substances in some plants are valuable in medicine when properly used.

The common Foxglove (above) is a herbaceous plant grown for its colourful flowers. It also contains digitalis, a substance which if taken in large doses, can cause death. But in the correct dosage, it is used as a medicine to regulate heart-beat.

The toxic substance contained in the sap of the Oleander is used to produce rat poison.

In the tuber family there are plants which are important to our diet, like tomatoes and potatoes. Some tubers are also poisonous. Almost all contain a poison called solanine in the leaves and unripe fruit. The Petunia (below) and the Tobacco Plant are also part of this family.

• HOW WHEN WHAT WHY •

What creatures feed on poisonous plants?

The grubs of the American Monarch Butterfly feed on Asclepias, a poisonous weed. The poison has no known effect on people, but it harms birds. So, if any bird daring to feed on the butterfly grubs soon regrets it! The result is that birds quickly learn to recognize the plant's bright colours and avoid it – leaving the grubs of the Monarch Butterfly in peace and safety.

WHAT IS A RAIN FOREST?

Nowhere else on Earth do plants grow so vigorously as in the hot and damp regions near the Equator, in the tropical rain forests. Each one is a very complex ecosystem (or nature community). More than half the total of living organisms on Earth live in the rain forests! Here, the tallest trees grow to more than 50 metres high and their branches extend all around for tens of metres. Closer to the ground, other trees thickly woven together form the undergrowth of the forest. Between the undergrowth and the ground, climbing plants, creepers, trees and bushes often make the forest impassable.

• HOW WHEN WHAT WHY •

Why do some sloths have a bluish haze?

In the thick fur of some species of sloth live colonies of blue algae which the animal finds useful as a disguise in the forest among the leaves and the mosses. The 'micro-climate' which is created by the sloth's fur is ideal for the growth of this algae!

LIFE IN THE TREES

Lots of mammals which live in the rain forests have adapted to life in the trees. They move from one plant to another in search of food.

- In the equatorial rain forest the average rainfall is 1500-1400mm every year. The temperature swings between 25°C and 35°C.
- In one hectare (100sq.m) of rain forest, it is possible to find between 80 and 200 different species of plants.
- The Amazon rain forest covers a large part of the equatorial zone of South America (around 6 million square kilometres).

WHICH PLANTS GROW IN THE RAIN FOREST?

The Mangrove grows in the water salt marshes at the mouth of rivers. Its roots descend from the branches to the water, creating wonderful arched structures, homes for tropical fish and birds.

Epiphytes are plants which grow on branches of other trees. Their roots hang free and absorb the moisture in the air. The orchid belongs to this plant family, as well as bromeliads, which includes the pineapple.

In the lower layer of the rain forest we find the habitat of ferns, which give shade and humidity.

WHICH PLANTS LIVE IN THE DESERT?

In the desert, plants must survive for long periods without water; that is why their roots go deep into the ground, where they can find moisture. Plants such as the cactus have thick stalks which can store water, and the leaves have a waxy covering to reduce evaporation to the minimum. A cactus also has spines to defend itself against animals. The seeds of some of these plants stay in the ground until a rare fall of rain. When they begin to grow, the plants germinate in a short time, flowering and then the fruits spreading new seeds on the ground.

● HOW WHEN WHAT WHY ●

What use are the spines in a cactus?

Cactus spines are actually modified leaves. As well as being a defence against animals, spines also limit the amount of water which evaporates into the air, because they only expose a limited surface to the heat of the Sun.
Spines can also collect night-time moisture in the air. This moisture condenses at their tips, then drips down the length of each spine and through the plant to the roots.

WHAT ARE SUCCULENT PLANTS?

'Succulents' are plants that can accumulate water inside the stem and their fleshy leaves. Cactus and succulents are widespread in the American deserts.

The Ferocactus is a long, round-shaped plant, with yellow, red and orange flowers. Its stem is covered with clusters of spines, like its fruit, the prickly pear.

AT RISK OF EXTINCTION

Some species of cactus are at the risk of extinction because they are much prized as plants in the cities. Not being protected, they are gathered indiscriminately by illegal collectors and traders.

- The leaves of an Agave can reach 2m in length and its flowers to a height of 10m.
- The Giant Saguaro cactus can reach heights of 15m with spines 7cm long.
- A cactus without arms (i.e. not the familiar 'chandelier') in Arizona, USA, has reached a record-breaking height of 24m, as tall as a 7-storey building!
- Some examples of the Ferocactus are 3m high.

EFFICIENT ROOTS

The roots of many desert plants can often extend sideways near the surface. In this way, the roots can also use the small amount of moisture left by the morning dew. Extensive side roots are the reason why plants grow far apart in the desert.

In the Equatorial African deserts lives the 'Stone Plant'. This plant gets its name because the tips of its stalks are like stones on the ground.

The fleshy leaves of the Agave, with its spiny edges and a prickle at each point, are able to collect remarkable quantities of water. The Agave flourishes just once in the course of its life, at the age of between 10 and 20 years. Then it withers and dies.

WHICH PLANTS LIVE IN WATER?

Some plants live completely under the water. Some float on the surface. Others grow in the water of ponds or on the banks of rivers and are partly covered by water. The plant Elodea (pondweed) has a long, strong underwater root which is anchored to the water bed. The stem and the leaves, which are on the surface, are thin, so that they are able to resist the wind without being 'uprooted'! The Water Lily floats on or lives underwater. The floating leaves have the stomata on the upper part exposed to the air.

THE WATER LILY
This plant flourishes near pools and lakes. The Fanwort grows around swamps. It has sausage-like flowers on a stalk which can be up to 2.5m long.

Want to see a plant breathing underwater? Put a water-plant in a jar full of water. Place a piece of card on top, then, holding the card in place, upturn the vase. Place the whole thing in a basin full of water. Slide out the cardboard carefully and put the basin and the jar in full sunlight. After a while, you will see lots of bubbles in the vase. These are bubbles of oxygen produced by the plant.

- There are at least 4000 species of red seaweed, 1500 species of brown seaweed and 6000 green seaweed.

- Some seaweeds of the Pacific Ocean grow a good 45cm each day, reaching approx. 60m in length.

- Green and brown seaweeds live at depths of no more than 25m, because they need sunlight. Red seaweed can live with very little light at depths more than 100m.

WATER PLANTS

The flower of the Water Lily closes during the night and opens out at dawn.
The Water Chestnut has floating leaves. Its spiny fruit looks rather like the seed-case of a horse-chestnut. The Water Buttercup (or Water-Crowfoot) has yellow flowers and long, pointed leaves.

WHAT ARE SEAWEEDS?

Seaweeds are very simple plant organisms which live in the sea and in fresh water. Some seaweeds are microscopic. These, together with tiny little water creatures called plankton, are food for fish. Many-celled seaweeds are anchored to the depths by a rhizoid, which is like a small, climbing root. Some species are sprinkled with small 'blisters' full of air, so they can remain upright in the water.

Red and brown seaweeds live in salt water, green seaweed mostly in fresh water.

143

WHY DO SOME PLANTS HAVE FLOWERS?

Flowers contain the plant's reproductive organs which have a most important task – to generate seeds to give life to new plants. The male organs of the flower, the stamens, produce pollen, which is made up of tiny little grains of powder, usually yellow. These grains of pollen, carried by the wind, by water or by animals, become 'intercepted' by the pistil, the female part of the flower, and these reach the ovary. Seeds form when the pollen comes in contact with an ovule – that is, when an ovule has been fertilized.

● HOW WHEN WHAT WHY ●

Why are flowers perfumed?

Flowers are perfumed because their petals contain essential oils, widely used in the manufacture of perfume. The oil of the rose, violet and jasmine are the ones most widely used, for medicines and disinfectants, as well as perfume. A flower's perfume also attracts pollinating insects, such as bees and wasps. However, there are some flowers which have an unpleasant smell. For instance, the Stapelia, in order to be pollinated, attracts flies with a smell of bad meat.

THE PISTIL

At the top of the pistil there is the stigma, a sticky swelling which catches the pollen. Below this is the style, along which the pollen descends towards the ovary at the centre of the flower.

WHICH ARE THE PLANTS WITHOUT FLOWERS?

Conifers reproduce by keeping their seeds in cones. These plants have male cones (the smaller ones) and female cones. The pine cone of the Conifer tree protects the little pines by its woody scales.

1) In which plants do you think the flowers grow before the leaves?
❏ Hibiscus   ❏ Forsythia   ❏ Petunia

2) Where do you think flowers do not grow?
❏ in the desert   ❏ in water   ❏ on ice

3) What is the collective name for all the petals in a flower?
❏ corolla   ❏ gemma   ❏ calyx

4) How many species of rose do you think there are?
❏ 30   ❏ 100   ❏ 250

5) What colour is the flax plant?
❏ white   ❏ red   ❏ blue

Answers
1) Forsythia 2) on ice
3) corolla 4) 250 5) blue

Stigma

Style

Ovary

Ovule

THE OVULE
The ovule is inside the ovary. It is here that the fertilization takes place to begin the development of new seeds. From this moment, the ovary is transformed into a fruit.

Ferns are reproduced by spores, microscopic cells which drop from the underside of the leaf. The spores germinate and develop into tiny, usually heart-shaped plants which contain the male and female cells ready to create a new plant.

Mosses reproduce by spores, too. These are contained in small capsules at the ends of steles, central tubes of the stems. Each spore can give life to a new plant.

145

HOW DOES A PLANT BEGIN LIFE?

Inside each seed, there is an embryo plant and a precious food store, ready for the first phase of the plant's life cycle. When conditions are right – when the ground is sufficiently warm and moist – the seed germinates. It sends out its main root, with other, smaller roots branching off. Then the first leaves appear. The plant is now complete and can continue to grow, feeding itself by using the sunlight.

IF THERE IS NO WATER…

If a seed disperses into dry surroundings, it does not die. Instead the seed stays in the ground for up to a year until there is contact with water. Then it begins to germinate. Once the plant begins to grow, the seed withers, because it is no longer required to feed the new plant.

• HOW WHEN WHAT WHY •

How is pollen spread?

When an insect lands on a flower searching for nectar, tiny grains of pollen stick to its feet or wings. So, when the insect flies to another flower, it deposits a little of this pollen on the stigma of the plant. Pollination is also carried out by the wind, or birds, like the Hummingbird.

Things · To · Do

Do you know how flowers can grow, even without soil? Put an Amaryllis bulb in a jar of water, so that the underside of the bulb is underwater. Place the jar in a shady place. Then, when the first leaves appear, put the jar in the light. You will see the bulb sending out roots and before long, a beautiful flower will appear. The food necessary for the plant is in the bulb.

How can a plant reproduce without seeds?

Some plants develop from bulbs or tubers – underground stems which can draw up the food necessary for new shoots. The part of the potato plant which we eat is the tuber. This tuber would have supplied food to the new shoots so that a new potato plant would grow.

Bulbs are made up of layers of leaves. These leaves protect the cells from which the new plant will develop.

Bananas do not grow from seeds. The roots of a new plant grow on a rhizome, an underground stem which grows horizontally, and nourishes the plant in the same way as a bulb or tuber.

Some plants such as strawberries produce shoots which grow sideways, called runners. On contact with the soil, these runners develop roots, giving life to a new plant. When the plant begins to grow, the runner withers and dies.

WHAT IS THE STRUCTURE OF A SEED?

Inside a seed is an embryo, a plant in miniature – a little root, the tiny little stalk which will grow above ground, always in the centre of the plant, and the embryo leaves, or cotyledons, which will nourish the plant until the actual leaves are able to produce food for themselves. Seeds which contain just one embryo leaf, such as maize, are called monocotyledons. Seeds containing two embryo leaves, such as the bean, are called dicotyledons. From these two types of seed originate plants with different characteristics.

A PROTECTIVE LAYER

The layer which covers the seed is called the testa. When this comes in contact with water, it swells, bursts and then separates from the seed.

Testa

● HOW WHEN WHAT WHY ●

Why do we eat the seeds of cereals?

The reserve foods in cereal seeds contain carbohydrate, fats and protein, all of which are important in our digestion and diet. Also, the outer part of the seed (the husk) is rich in cellulose, an important food fibre. Husk, mixed and ground with seeds of wheat, gives us wholemeal flour. Wheat, rice, barley, maize, rye and oats are all cereals.

FACTS·AND·FIGURES

• The largest seed in the world is the Sea Coconut, which grows only in the Seychelles. It can weigh up to 20kg.

• The smallest seeds are those of the Epiphytic Orchid. One million of these tiny, little seeds weigh only one gramme.

MONOCOTYLEDON PLANTS

These have upright leaves with parallel vein. Tulips, orchids, cereals such as maize, rice and barley and many vegetables such as the onion and the asparagus, the Palm Tree and the Banana Tree are all in this group.

DIOCOTYLEDON PLANTS

These plants have wide leaves with veins branching out. There are at least 200,000 different plant species in this group, including many vegetables, fruit trees, vines, olives, tea and coffee plants.

HOW ARE SEEDS SPREAD?

Seeds of plants are spread (or 'dispersed') in many different ways, some very unusual. Some seeds are dispersed by the wind. To help with this dispersal, some seeds like maple or lime have little wings. Others, like the dandelion, have a pappus, a ring of silky hairs which acts like a parachute.

Some seeds have little spines or 'burrs', so that they become attached to the skin of animals and are carried away.

Fruits are eaten by animals, then the seeds inside passed as waste material, some distance from the parent plant.

There are plants such as the poppy which, when the fruit is ripe 'fires' its seeds so that these land some distance away.

Other plants use water to disperse their seeds. The coconut is carried long distances by the sea waves.

WHAT ARE FRUITS?

In a flower, when the seeds develop, the petals fall off and the swollen ovary becomes transformed into a fruit, which in turn is protecting new seeds inside it. Some fruits are edible and rich in important vitamins. There are soft fruits, such as the peach, the plum and the pear, citrus fruits such as oranges, and dry fruits such as nuts. Even tomatoes are fruits.

WHICH PART OF THE VEGETABLE DO WE EAT?

The edible parts of vegetable plants are very different. From some, we eat the roots, from others, the stems, the leaves, the tuber or the bulb. In the cauliflower plant, the part we eat is the flower; in peas, we eat the seeds.

The carrot is a root

We eat the stem of celery, from the lettuce, the leaves.

The potato is a tuber

The onion is a bulb

• HOW WHEN WHAT WHY •

Where do we get nuts from?

Nuts are produced by green, fleshy plants which contain a seed protected by a woody shell. The part of the nut we eat is really the seed, or kernel. This is rich in a natural oil, and, like all dry fruits, is very nutritious.

WHICH ARE THE LARGEST PLANTS?

Trees are the largest plants. The Sequoia, for instance, has impressive dimensions, with a diameter measuring up to 9m. The largest Sequoia, 11m in diameter and 83m tall, is called the General Sherman and is in the National Sequoia Park in the USA. This tree is believed to be more than 2000 years old. The Australian Eucalyptus, with a height of 130-140m, is the tallest tree of all. The tree with the largest trunk, up to 10m in diameter, is the Baobab. The spread of its foliage can reach up to 80m in circumference.

The largest flowers in the world are those of the Rafflesia Arnoldii, (or 'Stinking Corpse' lily) a water lily without either stem or leaves and which grows, attached to other green plants, in the forests of Southeast Asia. Its gigantic flowers, red and white, have a diameter of about 90cm and can weigh up to 10kg!

The leaves of the Raffia Palm, a palm tree native to Madagascar in Africa, can reach up to 20m in length.

The gigantic water lily The Queen Victoria grows in Central America. Its thick, strong leaves can be up to 2m in diameter.

• HOW WHEN WHAT WHY •

What are the smallest plants?

In Canada, a White Cedar tree has grown only 10cm in 155 years! The smallest flowering plants in the world are the Rootless Duckweed, found mostly in Australia, and the Swamp Duckweed of Brazil. Both plants are similar to ordinary duckweed, but their flowers measure less than one millimetre in diameter.

HOW DO WE USE PLANTS?

All plants have an enormous importance in our food chain. They are also useful in the making of medicines, perfumes, cosmetics, textiles, paper, colourings and tools. We use different parts of the plant according to what we need. From the bark of some trees we can obtain cork. At one time, salicylic acid, an essential part of the medicine aspirin, was extracted from the bark of the willow. Now this acid is produced in laboratories. The leaves, the roots and the flowers of herbs are used for health purposes. We get wood from the trunks of trees, and rubber is made from the sap of the rubber tree. The seeds of the fruit of the cotton plant are wrapped in a fine down, used in the manufacture of cotton thread and material.

● HOW WHEN WHAT WHY ●

What are spices?

Spices are vegetable substances with a strong smell and taste, extracted from plants and used to prepare and to flavour foods. Many spices, such as pepper, cinnamon, saffron, cumin, aniseed and ginger are found in tropical plants. Aromatic herbs, such as mint, thyme and rosemary are widely used in cooking.

WHICH DRINKS COME FROM PLANTS?

The most widespread drinks in the world, tea and coffee, originate from plants. The tea plant is grown in tropical regions. The major producers are China, India, Indonesia, Sri Lanka and Japan. To obtain black tea, the leaves are first pressed, then left to ferment and dry out. To obtain green tea, they are first withered in steam and then dried.

PAPER-MAKING

Wood from the birch tree, the beech, fir, pine and spruce are used to make paper. First the wood is made into a pulp, then a paste, which is then transformed into sheets. These sheets are pressed and then dried.

1) *From which of these plants do we make beer?*
❏ wheat   ❏ birch   ❏ barley

2) *Which of these plants do not produce a textile fibre?*
❏ hemp   ❏ agave   ❏ banana

3) *From which part of the flax plant do we obtain an oil?*
❏ seeds   ❏ flowers   ❏ leaves

4) *From which plant do we get vanilla?*
❏ sugar cane   ❏ pineapple   ❏ orchid

5) *Which part of the breadfruit tree can be made into flour?*
❏ the bark   ❏ the leaves   ❏ the fruit

Answers
1) barley 2) agave 3) seeds 4) orchid
5) the fruit

WOOD FOR CARPENTRY

The wood of some trees, such as mahogany, oak, chestnut and rosewood are much sought after for their strength and their beauty. The wood is used in the making of furniture, floors and many other items.

The ripe red fruits of the coffee plant are dried and the flesh taken out. The beans are then toasted until they become the familiar brown colour.

The chocolate bean is used throughout the world in the preparation of drinks and sweets. The plant is grown in Africa and Central America. The fruit is crushed and then the seeds dried, toasted and ground.

How do plants defend themselves?

Fixed to the ground or to other plants, a plant cannot flee from danger. So to defend itself from animals, it has various means of protection. Some are covered with spines, like the rose, many grasses, and the Acacia tree in the tropical grasslands. Others plants can cause irritation, like the nettle, which stings on contact with the tiny, little needles that cover its leaves. The shy Mimosa curls up as soon as anything touches it. The Stone Plant disguises itself among the stones of the African desert.

● HOW WHEN WHAT WHY ●

How did the Sunflower get its name?

The Sunflower is a plant which is widespread throughout the world and famous for its peculiar behaviour, from which it gets its name. During the day, its bloom is always turned towards the Sun. Like all tropism phenomena, (turning towards a stimulus) the movement of the Sunflower is controlled by a hormone, a substance produced by the plant and which can stimulate or stop growth. This hormone is mainly in the part which is in the shade, and which grows more quickly than the part in the Sun, where there is less hormone. The Sunflower tries to balance this distribution by constantly bending its stem towards the Sun.

THINGS·TO·DO

Put some moist blotting paper around the inside of a jar. Between the glass and the paper, place some beans, and put the whole thing in a warm place. Wait a few days and you will see the beans sending down roots towards the bottom, and shoots towards the top. At this point, turn the jar sideways. After a few more days, you will see that the shoots and the roots have changed direction, and they are growing once again in a vertical direction.

TOO MUCH WATER
The leaves of some tropical plants have a special 'drain', like a gutter, so that the leaf can pour away a surplus of water after a lot of rain.

DEFENCE AGAINST THE COLD
To defend themselves against the cold, some flowers, like the Sunflower, turns its corolla, following the course of the Sun. In this way, the flower takes full advantage of the maximum warmth from the rays of the Sun.

ARE PLANTS SENSITIVE?
Plants, like animals, react to stimuli in their surroundings with movements called tropisms. Some flowers close at night and re-open at dawn.

The roots of plants always grow towards the bottom, sensitive to the force of gravity, whilst the shoots always grow in the direction of the light. Some roots also develop horizontally, in search of water or particular substances in the ground which they need.

Climbing plants are sensitive to contact. They cling to every possible thing that they touch.

155

HOW CAN WE TELL THE AGE OF A TREE?

Trees grow in height, in width and in depth. The trunk becomes thicker, adding a new layer of wood beneath the bark each year. These layer form concentric rings – and so, by counting these rings, we can find out the age of a tree. The thickness of each ring also indicates the weather conditions in which it grew. The rings are wider in the case of rain and sun, thinner if the tree has suffered drought.

- The oldest living tree is called Eternal God and is a Sequoia which has survived more than 12000 years.

- The highest number of rings counted on a felled tree was a Sequoia over 4000 years old and 280 each centimetre of rays.

- The most rapid growth of a tree was observed in a False Acacia in Malaya – 10 metres in 13 months.

- The oldest pine tree in the USA is 4600 years old.

HOW LONG DOES A PLANT LIVE?

The life cycle of an annual plant is just one year. Annuals include poppies, tomatoes, eggplants (aubergines), cereals and many other vegetables. Carrots, celery and rape are biennial plants, which means they complete their life cycles every two years.

Perennial plants live for more than two years. The crocus, iris and narcussus belong to this group. During the winter, their bulbs conserve the substances necessary for their rebirth in the spring. Many trees and bushes renew their life cycle each year, after having reduced their activity during the winter.

Science and Technology

WHAT ARE ATOMS?

Everything around us is made up of tiny particles of matter called atoms. Two or more atoms of the same or of a different type forms the molecule, which is the basis of each substance. For instance – a water molecule has two atoms of hydrogen and one atom of oxygen. Molecules of solid substances are bound together with a force which is very strong. The force which binds molecules of liquid is much weaker, and molecules in gases move in every direction. It was once thought that the atom was the smallest particle of matter. But scientists then discovered that atoms are made up of even smaller particles called electrons and protons, which each have an electrical charge. Electrons have a negative charge and move around the nucleus. Protons have a positive charge and are tied to the nucleus. Some atoms have neutrons which are also tied to the nucleus.

• HOW WHY WHEN •

Why does iron go rusty?

Rust forms on the surface of iron objects when these are exposed to the air. It is the product of a chemical reaction called oxydization. The more the object is exposed to the air, the more rapidly rust spreads. Once rust has formed, it makes the surface crumble, exposing the layers underneath to the air so that these too become rusty as a result of oxydization.

ORGANIC AND INORGANIC CHEMISTRY

Organic chemistry is the study carbon compounds. Carbon is one of the basic elements of living organisms. Inorganic chemistry is the study of chemical compounds.

• There are actually more than 200 sub-atomic particles.

• One grain of dust contains a billion atoms.

• One drop of water contains 10 billion water molecules.

• One molecule of hydrogen contains two atoms of hydrogen.

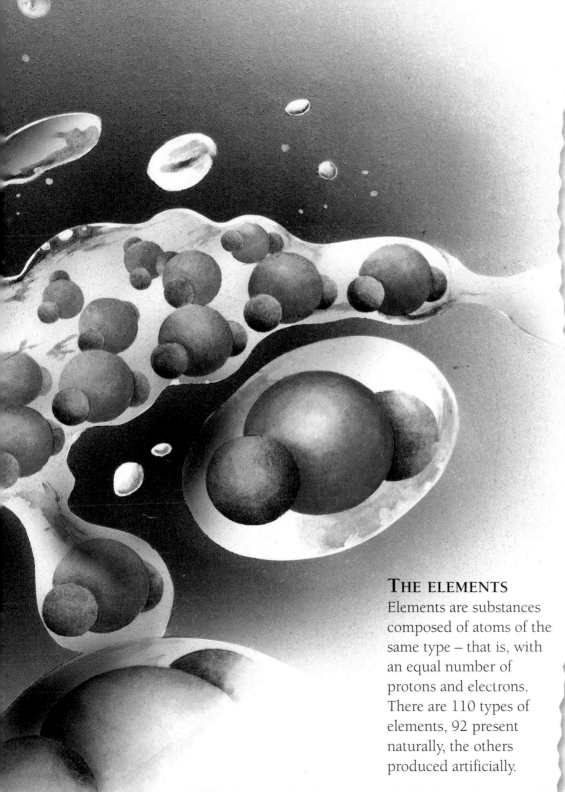

WHY DOES A SLICED APPLE GO BROWN AFTER A WHILE?

A chemical reaction can separate, unite or combine differently the elements which constitute a substance. A simple contact between two molecules can be enough for a chemical reaction. Other times it happens by the intervention of heat or electricity, or by a catalyst (an external factor which activates the reaction). In chemical reactions, matter is transformed, but not destroyed, nor is new matter created. A sliced apple goes brown due to the chemical reaction of oxydization – because the iron content in the apple combines with oxygen in the air.

THE ELEMENTS

Elements are substances composed of atoms of the same type – that is, with an equal number of protons and electrons. There are 110 types of elements, 92 present naturally, the others produced artificially.

WHAT MAKES A FLAME?

A flame is a bright, shining mixture generated by the combustion (burning) of a substance, either solid, liquid or gas. For a flame to burn, there must be three elements – 1) heat; 2) the combustive (oxygen); and 3) the combustible (a material such as wax or petrol, which can be burned). A match bursts into flame when the 'head' is at the right temperature for the oxygen to burn the sulphur. When we blow on the match, we reduce the temperature and so the combustion is interrupted.

THE REMAINS OF COMBUSTION

Smoke, cinders and soot are among the products of combustion. When a substance burns, it is not completely destroyed but is transformed into other substances and into heat.

• HOW WHY WHEN •

How do we measure the temperature of something?

There are many scales for measuring temperature, each one named after its inventor – Celsius, Fahrenheit, Kelvin and Rankine. The one commonly used in most countries is the Celsius Scale (C). Here are some examples:

250°C: temperature of the combustion of wood

100°C: temperature of boiling water

37°C: normal body temperature of a human

0°C: temperature of frozen water

-39°C: temperature of solidification of mercury

-273°C: absolute zero (complete absence of heat).

THE SHAPE OF A FLAME

A flame has an elongated shape, because the hot air is lighter than the cold air, and so the hot air rises upwards.

Try this simple experiment to prove that a flame goes out without oxygen. Take a candle and fix to a plate with a little piece of modelling clay. With the help of an adult, light the candle, then cover it with a glass jar. In a few moments, you will see the flame going out, because the oxygen in the jar will be used up.

WHAT IS A COMBUSTIBLE?

Substances which burn rapidly in the presence of oxygen and which give off large quantities of heat are called combustibles. Such substances are used to produce light, heat and energy. Combustible solids include firewood and coal. Benzine, gasoline and kerosene are all derived from petrol, a liquid combustible. Natural gas and methane are combustible gases.

WHY DOES LIGHTNING STRIKE?

Spectacular flashes of lightning are caused by short, violent transfers of electric charges, either between one cloud and another, or between clouds and the earth. During a thunderstorm, the lower parts of clouds (the parts nearest the earth) accumulate lots of negative electric charges – whilst, on the ground, positive electric charges accumulate. When there is a build-up of negative charges in the sky, these charges move towards the positive charges on the earth, and cause lightning. This in turn causes a further exchange of positive charges from the earth. What happens then is that the negative electric charges jump towards the upper parts of the cloud, which is when we see the lightning flashing upwards.

• HOW WHY WHEN WHO •

Who invented the Lightning Conductor?

The Lightning Conductor was invented by the American Benjamin Franklin in 1752. He built a kite with an iron tip, threaded a key (also of iron) at the bottom of the string, and flew the kite during a thunderstorm. Franklin proved that the iron tip attracted the lightning and carried the electric charge down the string to the key – in fact, Franklin got an electric shock by touching the key. Following the experiment, Franklin built his first Lightning Conductor, a steel mast which he placed a short distance from his house. The point of this Lightning Conductor attracted the stormy electric charges and dispersed these into the ground, avoiding any damage caused by lightning striking the building.

ATTRACTION

Opposite electric charges attract. Charges of the same repel. During a storm, the positive charges on the ground attract the negative charges in the clouds.

CHARGES IN MOVEMENT

Positive electric charges are enclosed within the nucleus, and so cannot move. Negative charges are outside the nucleus and so can be overcome or acquired. The atoms which are overcome remain with a larger number of positive charges. Those which are acquired will remain with more negative charges.

When something becomes electrified, it acquires the capacity to attract lightweight objects, acting rather like a magnet. To prove this, stroke a balloon with a piece of wool. The electrons of the wool pass on to the balloon. On the wool there will be positive charges and, because opposite charges attract, the wool and the balloon are drawn together. Now tie two inflated balloons at either end of a length of thread. Stroke a piece of wool on the balloons and hold the thread in the centre. You will see that the balloons draw apart, because they have taken the same type of (negative) charges from the piece of wool.

ELECTRIC CHARGES

Atoms are formed by some particles with negative electric charges and others with positive charges. When there is an equal number of charges, the atom is neutral.

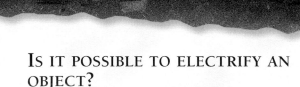

IS IT POSSIBLE TO ELECTRIFY AN OBJECT?

An object can be electrified by stroking it with a different material. For instance, a glass rod can be electrified by stroking it with wool. A moving car 'strokes' against the air and becomes charged with electricity. This phenomenon is temporary, because the electrical charges which accumulate are dispersed on contact with other objects. Have you ever seen little 'sparks' coming from your hair when you pull a sweater over your head? Or felt a tiny electrical shock by taking the hand of another person, or touching a car door? All these happen due to a sudden transfer of electrons from one electrified object to another – like flashes of lightning!

WHY DOES A LIGHT BULB GET HOT?

Light shines from an electric bulb because of the tungsten element inside it. The electricity enters the bulb along a filament, goes around the tungsten spiral and out through another filament. Tungsten is a metal conductor of electricity. But the spiral is so thin that it is hard for the electric current to pass through it. The force needed heats the tungsten spiral to the point where it results in light. And so the bulb gives off light and heat at the same time.

HOW DOES A TOASTER WORK?

Many things used in the home transform electrical energy into heat energy. Inside a toaster there are metal filaments, similar to those inside a light bulb. These heat up with the passage of an electrical current and so transform the electrical energy into heat. There are many other things which work in the same way – electric blankets, irons, hair-dryers and electric cookers.

● HOW WHY WHEN ●

Does electricity always produce heat?

In some cases, the heat produced by electricity is a problem, because it causes the dispersal and waste of part of the energy. Scientists have discovered that some metals, when cooled, do not resist the passage of the current, and so do not transform any of the electricity into heat. These metals called 'superconductors' are now widely used – for instance, in the construction of railway lines carrying high speed trains.

WHAT HAPPENS INSIDE AN ELECTRIC CABLE?

Electrical cables are 'canals' along which the current flows, connecting the different components of a circuit. Inside a cable there are thin filaments of copper which conduct the electricity. Copper, like other metals, has electrons which are free to move and therefore able to carry electricity from one point of the cable to another. Electrical cables are covered with plastic, a material that does not allow electricity to flow through. So we can touch the plastic covering of a cable without getting a shock.

HOW DO BATTERIES MAKE A RADIO WORK?

Batteries are like little supplies of electrical energy. Inside there is a chemical substance which can transform chemical energy into electrical energy. When we turn on a radio, the metal cap of the battery comes into contact with certain metal parts of the equipment; or, the internal composition of the battery creates a flow of electrons which generates the current. A battery is 'dead' when the composition inside is used up.

• HOW WHY WHAT WHEN •

What is an electric current?

An electric current is a passage of electrons from one electrified body to another which is less charged. When too many electrons are generated, they can move. For example – when we work a light switch, or switch on an electrical gadget on or off, we release some of the electricity stored in the central installation in the house, making it flow along the filaments until it reaches the gadget, or the light bulb.

WHY DO TWO MAGNETS SOMETIMES PUSH APART FROM EACH OTHER?

The two ends of a magnet are called poles. Each pole has a different electric charge (positive and negative). The positive pole of a magnet is always attracted to the negative pole of another magnet. But if two poles of the same charge are put near each other, the magnets push apart with a force of repulsion which can never be overcome.

MAGLEV TRAINS

Maglev (Magnetic Levitation) trains travel centimetres above the rails – because, instead of wheels, they have a system of magnets worked by electricity, the same as the rails. So as the same magnetic poles are pulled towards each other, they constantly repel (push apart).

• HOW WHY WHEN •

Why does the needle of a compass always point to the North?

The Earth is like a giant magnet. Its poles (North and South) produce a magnetic field which makes anything magnetic and movable point towards them. It is believed that this phenomenon is due to the steel and nickel in the nucleus of the Earth and also the rotation of the Earth which causes the rotation of the compass needle. The geographical North Pole and South Pole are not the same as the Earth's magnetic poles. In fact, the magnetic poles are some thousands of kilometres away from the geographical poles.

To magnetize a needle, find a bar magnet and two large needles. Stroke the magnet along each needle 40 times, always in the same direction. Then push one needle towards the other, first by the eye, then by the point. You will see that the needles act like two magnets, pulling together or pushing apart, according to which ends of the needles meet.

HOW DOES THE MAGNETIC COMPASS WORK?

A magnetic needle is fixed at the centre of a magnetic compass, on a pivot, so that it can rotate freely. The four cardinal points (north, south, east and west) are shown on the face, with the other geographical points in between. The needle always points to the magnetic North Pole, so that the other cardinal points can be calculated.

WHY DOES A ROLLING BALL GO DOWNWARDS?

If a ball is placed on a flat surface, it will only move by means of an external force – such as a kick or a gust of wind. But if the ball is placed on a slope, it will roll towards the bottom, moved by the force of gravity. If we roll a ball across a flat surface, we will see it slowing down after a while. This is because another force intervenes – friction against the ground, which slows down the movement of the ball until it stops. The friction comes from the contact between the surface of the ball and that of the flat surface.

TO 'HOLD' THE ROAD

If a car or bicycle were to go along on smooth tyres, they would not be able to 'hold' the road. The grooves in the rubber, that is, the 'tread', create a good friction with the asphalt and therefore enables the vehicles to 'hold' the road during curves and when braking.

TO TRAVEL FASTER

Although friction controls movement, in some cases it can reduce speed. That is why aircraft and speed-boats have pointed shapes, in order to reduce friction with the air and water and to travel at high speeds.

• HOW WHY WHEN •

Why does a sudden braking throw us forward?

When any method of transport stops suddenly, the passengers are thrown forward, as if they were still going on. If the transport starts suddenly, the passengers are 'pulled' back, as if they were wanting to remain still. Each body tends to remain inert – that is, to remain in the state in which it began. Therefore, it reacts in a manner contrary to the stimulus which changed its original state.

WHY CAN'T A BABY STAND ON ITS FEET?

If you have ever managed to balance a pen on your finger, you will have discovered its centre of gravity – that is, its point of balance. But if you move the centre of balance away, then the pen falls. In the human body, the centre of gravity is situated more or less under the tummy button. To remain in relation to our centre of gravity, our body is balanced on our feet, otherwise we cannot stand unaided. Small babies cannot stand on their feet because they cannot support their body weight and achieve the right balance.

WHY DO OUTSTRETCHED ARMS HELP BALANCE?

By stretching out the arms, the balance of the body is distributed differently and the centre of gravity remains above the base of support. Try getting up from a chair, keeping your feet in front of it and your arms by your sides. You will not be able to do it! But if you put your feet under the chair and move your arms forward, you will focus your centre of gravity on your feet once more and this will enable you to keep your balance and stand up.

● HOW WHY WHEN ●

Why do all cars have their engines mounted at the bottom?

To avoid becoming overturned easily, all vehicles are built in such a way that the centre of gravity is between the wheels. That is why the engine, the heaviest part of the car, is always at the bottom. If this weight were at the top of the vehicle, its balance would be at risk with each curve.

WHY DOES A ROAD RISING UPWARD HAVE LOTS OF CURVES?

To climb to the top of a mountain along a straight path, a mountaineer would need great physical strength. Also for cars, the force needed would be enormous. The curves in a mountain road make the journey longer, but this reduces not only the hard work of the climb but also the speed of ascent. So the winding road reduces the force necessary to complete a task. Tools which do the same are called simple machines.

SLOPING SURFACES
The curving road and the spiral staircase each reduces the force necessary to reach a height. In this way, they can be compared to simple machines.

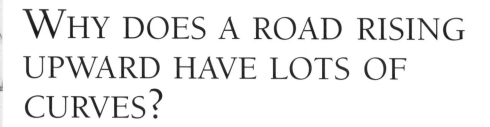

• HOW WHY WHEN •

How does a pulley work?

The pulley is a simple device which enables great weights to be lifted. It comprises a grooved disc or pulley which spins on a pivot fixed to a stirrup, around which passes a rope or a chain. At one end of the rope is fixed the item to be lifted, at the other is the person applying the force. To make the pulley work, a person uses his or her weight, pulling one end of the rope towards the ground, so that the weight rises up at the other end.

SCREWS

Imagine that the thread of a screw is a sloping surface. The screw penetrates into a surface with a spiral course, rising up vertically.

1) *Which tool simplifies the job of pulling a splinter from a finger?*

2) *Which simple tool consists of rotating teeth?*

3) *To raise the lid of a can, is it best to lever it off with a coin or with a screwdriver?*

4) *What is the positioning point of a lever called?*

Answers
1) tweezers 2) gear 3) screwdriver 4) pivot

FORCE MULTIPLIERS

A force multiplier is a simple machine which multiplies a small amount of human strength in order to move a load.

The corkscrew increases the strength of our hands. We can pull a cork out of a bottle, by pushing down the arms of the corkscrew.

The car jack enables a person to lift a car.

A crowbar is used to force open structures and objects which are stiff and resistant.

Nut-crackers do a job which would be too difficult for pure muscular strength.

All these simple machines are examples of force multipliers.

WHY IS A RAINBOW COLOURED?

The light from the Sun may appear white to us. But it actually consists of seven colours. If a beam of light crosses through the drops of water which remain suspended in the air after rainfall, it splits up into its seven colours and we see a rainbow in the sky. The same composition can be seen by making a beam of light pass through a glass prism. The colours of the rainbow always appear in the same order – red, orange, yellow, green, blue, indigo and violet.

ISAAC NEWTON

It was the English scientist Isaac Newton (1642-1727) who discovered that when crossing through a triangular prism of glass, 'white' light is split up into different colours.

• HOW WHY WHEN WHO •

Who invented the telescope?

The telescope is an instrument in which a concave mirror gathers in the light at one point called the objective, to produce an enlarged image. The first telescope was invented in Holland in 1608 by Hans Lippershey. Galileo improved on this and in 1609 built the first telescope to study the sky. This was made from a tube with a lens at each end. Modern telescopes owe their origin to the invention of the first reflective telescope by Isaac Newton (1668) which used mirrors in place of lenses, obtaining sharper images.

HOW DO LENSES CHANGE IMAGES?

The surface of lenses are curved. Therefore, they bend the rays of light which pass through them. Convex lenses make rays of light converge at one point. Concave lenses make rays of light spread out.

• The largest space telescope is the Hubble Space Telescope, put into orbit by a Space Shuttle in 1990. It has a mirror 24m in diameter weighing 11 tonnes.

• The smallest optical prism was made in a scientific laboratory in Colorado, USA, and is almost invisible, measuring 0.01mm.

• A normal microscope (with lenses and mirrors) can enlarge an element up to 2000 times, an electronic microscope more than one million times.

REFRACTION

The way in which a beam of light passing through a substance changes direction is called refraction. In the case of a rainbow, the light passes through raindrops, seeming to make the colours bend in the sky.

Convex and concave lenses are used in the manufacture of spectacles and other optical instruments, such as photographic machines, microscopes, projectors, binoculars and telescopes.

Rays of light, when they undergo refraction by a lens, create an enlarged or smaller image. Lenses used to examine small things, such as insects or postage stamps are convex.

WHAT IS A LASER?

A laser is a device which can generate a beam of light which is very fine and intense and can concentrate a large quantity of energy at one point. With its power and precision, the laser is now widely used for many tasks – cutting sheets of steel, welding metals, carrying out delicate operations in surgery, creating spectacular lighting effects in the sky, producing and reading compact discs, reading bar codes on products and many more.

The Big Book of
KNOWLEDGE

An interesting and informative book providing answers to many of the questions which intrigue young people.

Why does the wind blow? What is a galaxy? Do all animals care for their young? What did dinosaurs eat? Why do some plants have flowers? What are fibre optics?

Highlighted sections contain amazing facts and figures as well as quizzes and simple experiments.

Clear, easy to understand text, full colour illustrations and impressive photographs, guide the reader through the following subjects:-

Astronomy · Geology · Prehistoric Times
Atmospheric Phenomena · The Animal Kingdom
The World of Plants · Science and Technology

An enjoyable and invaluable source of information and reference for any young person!

ISBN 0-7097-1472-6

9 780709 714729 >

• HOW WHY WHAT WHEN •

What is a bank card?

A bank card is a magnetic pass stamped with the automatic code of the bank. Memorized in a magnetic strip on the pass is a small electronic circuit and usually, sometimes also in bar code, personal details of the owner, their secret code (PIN/Personal Identification Number) and details of the person's bank account. All this is fed to the withdrawal computer which then delivers the bank-notes to the cash dispenser and deducts the sum from the account.

WHY IS THERE A BAR CODE ON THINGS THAT WE BUY?

In most shops, all the information about a product (quantity in a packet, trade name, content, etc.) are memorized and processed by computer. The bar code contains information on the brand, the type of product, the contents and which elements distinguish the product from others which are similar. Price is not usually indicated, because this can change. When the bar code is seen by a laser scanner, this 'translates' the black and white bars into information. The white stripes reflect the light of the laser, the scanner transforms the light impulse into an electrical impulse and transmits this to a computer.

How does a compact disc contain sound?

The surface of a compact disc is aluminium, coated in transparent plastic. The metal disc underneath has grooves scored by a laser. Each groove is made up of microsocopic 'dots' which have a digital code representing the sounds. When we insert a CD into a player, a low-power laser beam is directed on to the rotating disc. The grooves and the flat parts on the surface reflect the light in different ways, creating a particular sequence of light impulses which are then read by a sensor and transformed into sound.

What is a DVD?

DVD stands for *Digital Versatile Disc.* It looks rather like a compact disc, but can contain a far larger quantity of data and can read at a much faster speed. One DVD video can input between two to eight hours of images and sound at the highest definition. One DVD can contain the original version of a film, different versions in other languages or with sub-titles.

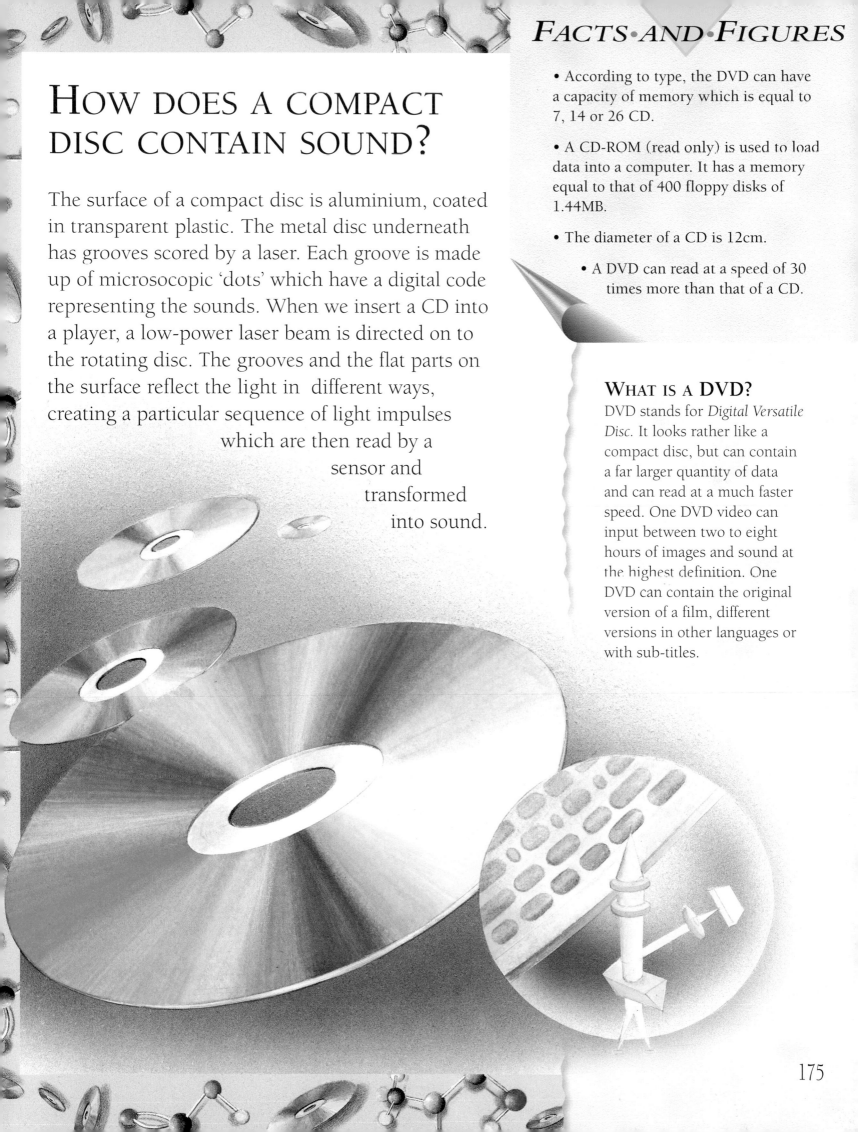

WHAT ARE FIBRE OPTICS?

Fibre optics are very fine filaments of transparent glass covered with a plastic material which makes them flexible and resistant. They are used to illuminate and to observe places which are not easily reached (inside the human body, for example) or to transmit coded information in the form of light signals (for example, in telephonic network or in those televised via cable). Due to the high speed of transmission (approximately two or three times the speed of light) and the ability to transfer a remarkable volume of information, fibre optics are the method of communication for the future.

FIBRE OPTICS AND MEDICINE

Fibre optics are used to look inside the human body. Because they are so fine and flexible, they can reach parts of the body which could not otherwise be reached without surgery. Fibre optics can illuminate a part of the body and transmit images to the doctor who can see these on a separate, external screen.

• HOW WHY WHAT WHEN •

What is a mirage?

Rays of light also undergo a distortion when they pass from warm air to cold air, or vice versa, because of their different density. On very hot days, the air near the ground heats up very quickly, and the rays of light which pass through the hot air becomes distorted. That is why to our eyes the road appears damp – but, in fact, we are seeing the reflection of the sky. This type of reflection can also make something appear to be upside down, or create the illusion of a mirror image of a reflection of water. This phenomenon is called a mirage.

FACTS·AND·FIGURES

• In electric cables, a signal can travel a distance of 1.5km, then it needs to pass through a relay in order to proceed on its way.

• In a fibre optic, signals can travel up to 100km before needing a relay.

• At a British University a fibre optic was made 10km long and with a thickness of 0.00000001mm, the finest fibre optic in the world.

HOW DOES LIGHT TRAVEL?

Light travels in a straight line. Because a fibre optic is like a tube with reflective walls, the light is imprisoned, rebounding from one point to another and therefore moving in very short, straight lines.

In fact, light changes direction when it passes through one material to another or when it meets a reflective surface, such as a mirror.

The light 'bends' a drinking straw to our eyes, by changing direction as it passes from the water to the air. Therefore the part of the straw which is under the water appears displaced from the part above the water.

The reflection you see in a mirror is the light reflected from your face hitting the mirror, bouncing off and then reaching your eyes.

WHY CAN'T AN AEROPLANE STOP IN MID-FLIGHT?

When an aeroplane flies into the sky pushed by the force of its engines, the air flows rapidly over its wings. Beneath the wings, the air slows down, because of the way the wings are curved. This creates a different force of pressure on the underside of the wing, which results in an upward push to sustain the aircraft. This upward thrust is called 'lift'. If the aircraft had to stop in flight, it would cancel out this difference in force between the air above the wing and the air below and the aircraft would crash.

REFUELLING IN THE AIR
Because aircraft cannot stop in the air, fuel tanks must be refilled whilst flying. This is especially important in particular situations, such as war, when aircraft cannot refuel on enemy territory and so has to cover long distances without stopping.

THINGS·TO·DO

Cut a strip of thin paper, about 10cm x 20cm. Hold it beneath your lips, and blow on the top surface. You will see that the paper does not bend down as you blow, but rises up. This is because the air flowing across the upper part of the strip exerts a lesser pressure than that which is exerted by the surrounding air. It is this pressure which makes the paper rise up – just like the air supporting the wings of aircraft.

WHAT WILL THE AIRCRAFT OF THE FUTURE BE LIKE?

Scientists predict that the aircraft of the future will have supersonic speeds. It will be possible to fly from Rome to Los Angeles in less than 4 hours, instead of the 10 hours flying-time today. There will also be new solutions for the comfort and safety of passengers. Aircraft of the future will have an increasing number of instruments for the prevention of accidents. It will also be possible to pilot an aircraft to the ground using new and sophisticated communication technology, thus eliminating the 'human factor' which can sometimes put aircraft safety at risk.

HELICOPTERS

Helicopters can stay in one place in flight, by means of the rotating movement of their blades. These spin rapidly in the air, creating a power capable of sustaining the helicopter. The shape of the helicopter blades are similar to that of an aircraft's wings and so can produce 'lift'.

HOW DO SUBMARINES RISE TO THE SURFACE?

Submarines reach the depths of the oceans by filling tanks with water. When they want to surface, this water is let out of the tanks and replaced by compressed air. These two operations allow the submarine to vary the level of immersion by the quantity of air present in the tanks.

• HOW WHY WHEN •

How is it that ships float?

An object immersed in water receives an upward thrust, equal to the weight of the water that object moves. This is called the Archimedes Principle. Because of their shape, ships move enormous quantities of water and so receive an upward thrust sufficient to make them float. But staying afloat also depends on a material's density – that is, the relationship between its weight and its volume. A ship is built of dense materials, like steel, but inside there are hollow cavities, full of air. These make the density of the ship less than that of the water, and so it keeps afloat.

WILL IT BE POSSIBLE TO LIVE AT THE BOTTOM OF THE SEA?

There are architects and town planners who are studying the possibility of installing underwater bases and laboratories, connected to the surface by a complex system of cables.

• The fastest speed recorded by a craft at sea is that reached by a USA war hovercraft SES-100B at 170km per hour.

• USA nuclear submarines have been designed to cover distances of 640,000km without being refuelled.

• The largest sailing ship is the *Sedov*, in the service of the Russian Navy. It is 109m long and 14.6m wide.

DOUBLE HULL

The hull of a submarine is usually double – the internal hull to withstand the pressure of water; the external hull has a shape perfect for navigation.

Before the dream of people living under the oceans can become a reality, solutions will need to be found to overcome problems such as isolation, climate and lack of sunlight so that people can live happily and safely whilst being able to explore their surroundings.

HOW DOES A VIDEO GAME WORK?

Every day, when we use the radio, the television, the computer or when we go into a shop with an automatic door, we put various electronic devices into action. Inside hand-held video games are miniaturized gadgets. The electric current does not flow constantly through these, as in an ordinary piece of electronic equipment, but is modified in signals. The video game transforms the mechanical signal (the touch from your finger), into a magnetic signal which makes it follow another on the screen (the images on display) in a continuous succession of signals going in and coming out.

ELECTRONIC CIRCUITS

Electronic circuits have components such as resistors, condensers, diodes and transistors. A single circuit can contain hundreds of miniaturized components which regulate the way in which the electricity is used. These components can amplify, activate, de-activate or turn off the equipment.

● HOW WHY WHAT WHEN ●

What is the 'language' of micro-chips?

The 'language' of the micro-chip is the binary code, which comprises just two signals, 'on' and 'off', which is translated as '1' and '0' like an alphabet of only two letters. Each piece of information which is entered into a chip, whether it is a sound, a drawing or a word, is converted into this code.

WHAT IS A MICRO-CHIP?

A micro-chip is truly microscopic in size – just a few square millimetres. But it is a complex electronic gadget capable of carrying out numerous and complicated functions inside televisions, telephones, computers. The micro-chip is mounted on a tiny, thin layer of silicone, which is a semi-conductive material, enclosed in a rigid, protective covering and connected to the equipment by little 'feet'.

One piece of electronic equipment can use numerous micro-chips, each with a specific function. In a telephone, for example, one micro-chip has the job of memorizing telephone numbers. Another records messages, others generate messages to appear on a screen, or transform signals into sound. The more electronic components in a chip, the more powerful and faster the equipment.

WHERE CAN WE USE A COMPUTER?

The constant development of communication systems has led to many of us taking part in debates by computer and playing games with people far away. We only have to go into a library or internet café to send electronic messages almost anywhere in the world. By way of a telephone line, the computers, connected together, form small and large networks. A school network allows all students to use the same information through different computers. The Internet connects computers worldwide, reducing distances between people and allowing the exchange of an enormous amount of information.

WWW

This means World Wide Web and indicates the multimedia system of information which can be accessed via the Internet – that is, across a network of computers connected on a world level.

• HOW WHY WHAT WHEN •

What is a video conference?

People far apart can 'meet together' to discuss topics concerning their work, or to study whilst remaining seated in front of the computer. Images and sounds can be transmitted by tiny tele-cameras and microphones placed on top of the computer monitor of each person taking part, so that everyone can see who is speaking.

184

FACTS·AND·FIGURES

- In 1995, there were 5 million computers connected to the Internet. At the end of 1998, it was more than 100 million – but this number is continually increasing and in the next few years, a 'growth explosion' is forecast.
- The USA is the country with the highest number of subscribers connected to the Internet – more than 50% of the total population.
- Sales of the Microsoft Flight Simulator game have exceeded 21 million copies.

WHAT IS VIRTUAL REALITY?

Virtual reality is a 3-dimensional environment, constructed electronically by computer. The user enters into the environment by wearing a helmet equipped with visualizers over the eyes. Computer-created images and sounds give users the sensation of actually moving within the place they see. The technology of virtual reality can be used not only in leisure (e.g. interactive video games) but also for professional purposes. For instance – doctors can gain experience of difficult surgical operations before they actually do them; pilots can carry out an emergency landing without risk, thanks to simulated flying practice. Architects can 'enter' a stately home, or illustrate a project before it is built. The gadgets to access any virtual surroundings can even be connected into the hands of a subscriber (by means of a special 'data glove') or to the whole body, by a special overall.

THE BIRTH OF THE INTERNET

The system of connecting computers on a network was developed for military purposes in 1969, by the Department of Defence of the USA. Then it extended into large corporations and research organizations. Today, millions of people worldwide are connected to the Internet.

CAN ROBOTS THINK?

Robots are automatic machines which can help people to do complex and repetitive tasks. A robot can work a through a computer which is already programmed, but cannot work independently. There have been studies and research with the aim of developing the robot's ability to interact with its surroundings. Some robots can already adapt their work with a reduced number of external stimuli. Although there will never be a robot which can 'think', some can react to unexpected stimuli and interact with people.

• HOW WHEN WHY •

How does a robot work?

Until now, no robot can function independently. It must always depend on the external control of a person. There are three phases in the function of a robot : 1) an external computer gives the instructions; 2) a motor makes the robot move; 3) other internal gadgets, called sensors, regulate and correct the robot's movements. There are some robots guided by a person, and which, in an environment of virtual reality, can simulate the actions necessary and transmit them.

WHAT CAN A ROBOT DO?

Robots are widely used in industry to help people in jobs which are tiring, dangerous and which need particular precision. In the car industry, robots cut and weld bodywork parts, or varnish different pieces. In the electronics industry, a robot can assemble different components.

FACTS·AND·FIGURES

- The largest robot was built for the film *Jurassic Park*. It housed a model Tyrannosaurus Rex 5.5m tall and 14m long.

- The robot PUMA, built in Switzerland in the 70s, is the most widely used in industry and in laboratories.

- The country with the highest number of robot installations (more than 300,000) is Japan.

- The robot *Zeus,* produced by the USA, is used for delicate operations in heart surgery.

FAMOUS ROBOTS

Some robots, created from the fantasy of directors, have become as famous as film stars – such as C3-PO and R2-D2 in *Star Wars* and Hal 9000 in *2001, A Space Odyssey.*

CYBERNETICS

Cybernetics is the science which studies the realization of machines capable of simulating the actions and behaviour of people.

A small, six-wheel robot, *Sojourner,* has been used in the exploration of the planet Mars. Other robots have been used in dangerous operations, such as defusing bombs or moving dangerous materials, and for precision work in surgery.

INDEX